T0277613

black
friend
Essays

♥
ziwe

ABRAMS IMAGE, NEW YORK

Editor: Holly Dolce
Designer: Diane Shaw
Managing Editors: Glenn Ramirez and Lisa Silverman
Production Manager: Sarah Masterson Hally

Library of Congress Control Number: 2021932581

ISBN: 978-1-4197-5634-4
eISBN: 978-1-64700-385-2
Text copyright © 2023 Ziwe Fumudoh
Jacket © 2023 Abrams

Printed and bound in the United States
10 9 8 7 6 5 4 3 2 1

Abrams Image books are available at special discounts when purchased in
quantity for premiums and promotions as well as fundraising or educational use.
Special editions can also be created to specification. For details, contact
specialsales@abramsbooks.com or the address below.

ABRAMS The Art of Books
195 Broadway, New York, NY 10007
abramsbooks.com

"they paying me, mama
  i should be paying them
  i should be paying y'all, honest to god"

—ziwe singing along to frank ocean in the car

contents

introduction

Today, I learned that my book is ranked as the #1 new release in "Discrimination and Racism" on Amazon. Wow. This is a huge honor, especially considering my stiff competition in the self-published manifestos space. Unfortunately, this victory is bittersweet. I worry that people may get the wrong idea and think that I am pro-racism when in actuality, I am indifferent. Still, I'd love to thank everyone who made this possible. I solemnly swear to write the most discriminatory book in American history. I hope I can make you proud.

Just kidding . . . I will not marginalize you . . . unless that's your kink. This book of essays offers moments of extreme discomfort (and the subsequent growth) in my life around the role of "black friend." Black friends come in all shapes and sizes. Yet the archetype is often a two-dimensional character meant to support the non-black protagonists' more complex humanity. Some black friends exist as the comic relief, like Donkey in any of the *Shrek* movies. Some are the sassy friend, like Louise from St. Louis in *Sex and the City*. Still others are the inexplicably sagacious companion, like Morpheus in *The Matrix*. It's impossible for these individual portraits to reflect my complicated reality. To start, they are fictional.

One of them is a talking ass. I do not exist just to move plot. While I am a supportive friend, I am not a supporting character. I am the protagonist of my perfectly imperfect story.

However, being the main character has its drawbacks. There is no one to hide behind. I would not be here if I did not fail—boldly, spectacularly, and with frequency. Sometimes in private, but too often in public. Failure has not killed me. Yet I am afraid of the vulnerability that comes with centering myself in my own stories. With limited representation comes the obligation to represent the entire black friend community. But black friends are not a monolith. While I pray that masses of readers/consumers connect to my hilarious AND thought-provoking essays, I can only speak for one black friend in particular: me!

Thus, I would like to lower your expectations on the depth and breadth of Amazon's #1 "Discrimination and Racism" book of essays. Yes, I will ask hard-hitting questions. Though, I should note, I do not have the answers. Consider this writing an examination of American identity politics if the term "identity politics" means "a black woman named Ziwe's shameless promotion of her own self-interests." Please, take every word I say with a grain of salt. I am fragile, as I subsist on an entirely ice cream–based diet.

More than anything, I aim to make you laugh and think, because that is what friends are for.[1] This is my goal in everything that I create, but especially in this book. This is *Black Friend*.

---

1   There are many opinions in this book, some that I will stand by until my dying breath, and others that I forgot I ever held immediately after typing them. Much like Walt Whitman, I contradict myself. But unlike Whitman, I am not a racist.

nobody knows my name

Ziwe: Hi, Rose. It is so nice to talk to you. You are so powerful.

Rose McGowan: *I am so—oh, thank you, Zeewee. You're fucking hilarious and genius. So there you go.*

Ziwe: Thank you, Rose. I have to correct you because you will get dragged in the comments for mispronouncing my name. It is Ziwe.

Rose McGowan: *I am so sorry. I haven't heard it said out loud. Ziwe?*

Ziwe: It is okay. I forgive you because of your contributions to cinema.

Rose McGowan: *Thank you.*[2]

People have mispronounced my name all my life. *Zeewee. Kiwi. Zigh-way. Highway. Zee Only Way.* Having to smile as someone makes another unoriginal pun about my name has created wrinkles that not even the most concentrated injection of Botox by Dr. Miami could fix.

---

2   Excerpt from interview with Rose McGowan, July 2, 2020, on Instagram Live.

I started going by just "Ziwe" as a performer because of oppression. When I tell people I am a mononym, it elicits eye-rolls that seem to say, "Who does this girl think she is?" But I began going by "Ziwe" because people develop short-term memory loss when you say a name that doesn't align with Western linguistic hits like "Smith" or "Johnson" or "Roald Dahl." Yet, when I first started doing live shows, I can't count how many times a host asked me how to pronounce my last name right before I walked onstage and then proceeded to introduce me incorrectly anyway. Even when I used mnemonic devices to demonstrate how easy my last name is to pronounce, they'd say something like, "Please welcome Ziwe Foomongdog." And then my whole set would start off on a bad note. *It's Fumudoh. My last name is phonetic.*

Another reason I identify as a mononym is that I do not like to have conversations about my name and how "special" it is. And if being a mononym puts me in the same conversation as Beyoncé, Madonna, and Prince, so be it. If anything, the fact that the ethnic name that I was tortured over can now be exploited for branding purposes is a form of reparations.

The problem with having an ethnic name is that whenever I introduce myself, people ask me too many questions. Where does it originate from? Nigeria. How do you spell it? Z-I-W-E. Do you know how beautiful your name is? Thank you, I'll tell my parents that you send your regards. This makes my interrogators laugh. Most of these people think they are being polite, not realizing this is most certainly the third or fourth interview about my name that I have endured that day.

But none of these questions exhaust me quite like when people ask, "What does your name mean?" Ordinarily when I get this question, I just lie and say, " 'Ziwe' means 'flower.' " This shuts people up very quickly, proving my theory that most people are too trusting when they ask for translations. I believe this is how tourists end up with Japanese tattoos that should mean "Your eyes are stars" but actually say "Beep beep lettuce." Personally, I have never been curious about the linguistic origins of "Jack" or "Sarah" or "Taylor," so I do not understand why anyone would care about the root of "Ziwe." Hmm. Maybe I am just defensive.

I was twenty-six years old when I learned the true meaning of my name. When [REDACTED] became president, I thought I should try to connect with my parents more before the internment camps started really popping off.[3] All my life, whenever I asked my mother what my name meant, her mind would wander and she would apologize and explain that when I was born my father was away. As a child with undiagnosed attention deficit disorder, this was enough to get me to move on. But as a twenty-six-year-old searching for meaning and ancestral connection, I decided to resume my pursuit of answers. One day, I called my mother and asked her for what was the thousandth time, "What does my name mean?" Like every other time, she apologized. But I continued.

"Okay, but what does my name mean?"

"That is what your name means."

---

3   If you think that is dramatic, then you really do not know much about our nation's love of camps! And I do not mean the fun camps. I am just saying—we live in a beautiful country that loves freedom, particularly the freedom to, on multiple occasions, detain religious and racial minorities.

"That is what my name means, what?"

"When you were born your father was away."

And then there was silence.

In that moment, what my mother had been telling me for years finally clicked. My mother was telling me that my name meant "born while your father was away."

"That is very disappointing."

"Yes."

If you were alive during the nineties/early aughts, you'll remember that twins were the most powerful beings on earth. I'm sure that the twin lobby secretly ran Hollywood to ensure their over-representation, because every network had a series centered on two people who looked alike switching places for comedic effect. From *Sister, Sister*'s Tia and Tamera Mowry, to *Two of a Kind*'s Olsen twins, to *The Suite Life of Zack & Cody*'s Dylan and Cole Sprouse, having a twin was the most valuable currency one could inherit.

I was not born a twin. I was just Ziwe. And unlike Lindsay Lohan, who manufactured a sibling and acted opposite herself for *The Parent Trap*, I would have to settle for the numerous black people that my teachers and employers thought I looked like. The only thing worse than being the only black person[4] in a room is being

---

4   This happens to all people of color. I stand in solidarity with you, Amy; I mean Alli.

one of two black people in a room who look nothing alike, constantly being misidentified by everyone around them.

The first time I can remember this happening to me was in third grade, when my teacher identified me as Kumbaya Kalvin,[5] the only other black girl in class. She was taller than me. She had hit puberty. She was more popular than me (see: puberty), and, again, we looked nothing alike. I was just Ziwe and she was *Kumbaya Kalvin*. I was too young to understand microaggressions, so I simply noted that I was not Kumbaya Kalvin, which prompted my teacher to ask if the only two black students in her class were sisters.[6] Would this not have come up during PTA meetings? The answer was obviously no . . . Kumbaya went on to clarify that the way to tell the difference between her and me was that she was related to Martin Luther King Jr. and I was not. What a creative lie. I respect her industriousness at such a young age. Everyone believed her, but the question remains: What was Martin Luther King Jr.'s great-granddaughter doing in a North Shore public school??? I knew she was a liar, but my peers were not only ignorant for thinking that black people looked alike but also stupid for believing that all black people were related.

As an adult, I learned that this was not an ignorance unique to the suburbs of Boston. Right before the pandemic, I did a lot of solo traveling in Europe because I read that James Baldwin had found inspiration in Paris. Much like Baldwin, I learned that every country offers its own unique and surprising interpretation of racism.

---

5 This is not her name because I do not want her to be doxxed, but it is something in this alliterative wheelhouse.

6 We were not sisters in the traditional sense! More like . . . sistas . . .

Racism is like a box of chocolates: You never know what you're going to get. In some countries and on one very specific continent, no one pays much attention to the fact that you are black, because everyone else is black. In other countries,[7] you are the first black person that locals have ever seen. They respond by treating you like an alien that they point and gawk at as you pass through public spaces.

Most places I've traveled are an unhealthy average of the two extremes. When I was in Rome, strangers frequently came up to me to ask me if I was Rihanna or Michelle Obama. Neither of these black women shares any resemblance with me (although I do have great arms). Anyone with vision sees that Rihanna and I are different shades of brown and sexiness. And anyone with knowledge knows that former first lady Michelle Obama is not getting drunk in the village of Regello without Barack Obama and a massive security detail. To be clear, I am not saying that anyone was racist, simply that when I visited the gorgeous northern countryside, I experienced treatment by the locals that was almost entirely based on my race. Whenever I would say no, they would get really disappointed and I would get horrible service. So I started saying yes, which led to maybe a dozen townies with photos in their camera roll of who they think is Rihanna but is actually just me, Ziwe.

The people I interacted with recognized that I was foreign and had a disposable income. To them, I was either international pop star and entrepreneur Rihanna or a brilliant dignitary who was also my

---

7   When my high school roommate went on a foreign exchange program to [REDACTED], she said that all the locals followed her around and called her the n-word ... or what she thought was the n-word but was actually the word for "black" in their native language.

mother's age, Michelle Obama. It was a binary that allowed locals to understand how to treat me and where I fit in their ecosystem. Otherwise, I guess they did not care to learn my name.

The last time this happened to me publicly was at the New York Liberty playoff game at Barclays Center. I love free stuff, so when the VIP influencer from the team reached out to me with courtside tickets, I jumped at the chance to attend a game. Also, that week I had just finished editing an interview with Michael Che, where he insisted that no one attends WNBA games. I wanted to prove him wrong, because the truth is I had never attended a WNBA game.

> **Ziwe:** *Name five WNBA players.*
>
> **Michael Che:** *Oh, I don't watch WNBA. I would love to watch it. But, WNBA, if you're watching this, if you're watching me, first of all, thank you. Second, if you got tickets, I would love to go to a game so I can learn more about your sport and culture.*
>
> **Ziwe:** *Uh, the sport is basketball.*
>
> **Michael Che:** *[laughs] Well, I mean, it's, it's a different . . . Yeah, I know about basketball, but I don't . . . Oh—*
>
> **Ziwe:** *It's different when—*
>
> **Michael Che:** *I don't like this. [laughs]*
>
> **Ziwe:** *When women dribble, it's different?*
>
> **Michael Che:** *It's, uh . . . It's . . . Yeah, it's different. Of course it's different. I think women and men are different, right?*
>
> **Ziwe:** *Can you describe their differences?*
>
> **Michael Che:** *Well, their ball is smaller. Right? Is it not? And there's no dunks, I know that much.*
>
> **Ziwe:** *[GASPS]*

Michael Che: *All right, whatever. Fucking breaking news, nobody watches the WNBA.*

Ziwe: *Oh my gosh!*[8]

I had a great experience. I was ushered in a side door for celebrities. I was escorted to courtside seats for celebrities. I was taken to a private club that had a pool inside Barclays Center for celebrities. I felt like a full-fledged celebrity, which I rarely feel like because I am not Rihanna, Michelle Obama, or someone who leaves my house for anything other than work. Attendants asked to take photos with me, and fans in the crowd shouted my name as I waved from a distance, wearing a mask, sunglasses, and overalls that said "ZIWE" on them. My friend and I were transferred from our first handler, who helped us enter the facility, to our second handler, who helped us to our seats. Part of being a celebrity is never having an unsupervised moment, because people genuinely fear you'll get lost and fall into a well. While seated, I was informed by our first handler that "at the end of the third quarter, we're going to show you on the jumbotron."

I was excited. This would be my first time as a celebrity on a jumbotron. I thought through my poses. Was waving basic? Yes. Should I take off my mask? No. I was wearing one to protect me from the "disease" of not putting makeup on that day. I hadn't yet settled on a pose when my credits started to play, including an elaborate trailer of season two of *ZIWE*. It was the female empowerment clip that was perfect synergy for the Women's National Basketball Association. After all, I was there to empower women.

---

8 Excerpt from interview in *ZIWE* S2 E7, "Men," November 18, 2022, on Showtime.

... Which is why I was surprised when as the jumbotron and announcer read ZIWE FUMUDOH, the cameraman was two feet beside me pointing at a different black friend. This was another famous black lady late-night host, Sam Jay of HBO's *Pause with Sam Jay*, who emphatically screamed, "No, I am not Ziwe! I am not Ziwe! I am not Ziwe!" as the announcer cheered, "It is ZIWE!!!" Soon, texts started rolling in about this misidentification, proving Michael Che wrong: People did in fact watch the WNBA.

I left the game early. Not because of the slight, but because the Liberty were losing and I wanted to beat traffic. Both of my handlers profusely apologized to me as people with taste cheered my name on the way out. I wish I could say that I was humiliated and outraged by this, but I was not. I was surprised because literally I did nothing to get myself there. A handler offered me free tickets. A handler walked me into the stadium. A handler sat me in my assigned seats. The jumbotron played clips of me that I did not send. I was wearing overalls that said "ZIWE." To mistake me for the other black woman who is sitting courtside takes several layers of error. Friends asked me if I had planned this moment as a publicity stunt, when in actuality this is just the culture around blackness in public spaces. The only thing that was planned was that we were following a rubric that I had been interacting with since I was in third grade with Martin Luther King Jr.'s *fugazi* granddaughter. The irony came from me being there to support women and unexpectedly being dehumanized in the process.

But in the words of Kourtney Kardashian, "Kim, there's people that are dying." Sure, as a celebrity, it should hurt my ego, but the following week, at the US Open, Laverne Cox was mistaken for Beyoncé and Dionne Warwick was mistaken for Gladys Knight.

What is uncommon for celebrities is everyday life for any black person. It just so happens that I am a regular black person who is also a celebrity. It is a statistical improbability that I am misidentified at the celebrity event to which I am invited as a celebrity, but black people get confused for each other all the time. I am not trying to normalize this problematic encounter. Rather, I want to convey the normalcy of it. Is it that your subconsciousness is not registering my name or my face because you do not deem either as worth knowing? Must I reiterate my identity in every room I walk in, even when I am invited? Even the inquiries in Italy seemed to me a way to validate whether I was a black woman of importance or just another black face.

On my way out, a father stopped me to take a photo with his young daughter. He said that even though she was too young to understand my show, she liked watching it because I looked like her. I crouched down and put my hands on her lil' shoulders and told her she could be anything she wanted to be, like Ziwe or not; she just had to believe it without seeing it.

A week after the WNBA game, I attended the US Open with a friend. As we entered, her handler mentioned that he was a fan of my show. I told him that he was a man with taste. I enjoy attending events with her because I get to observe what extreme fame is like for attractive white women with equally difficult names. There is no anonymity with her. During the match, they showed her on the jumbotron. Then, to my surprise, they cut to me—and announced "ZIWE." I waved, which was basic, but it was the only thing I could think of in that instant. I was delighted. Not because they recognized me, which was nice, but because they knew my name was just Ziwe.

airbnb

Ziwe: *How many black friends do you have, Caroline?*

Caroline Calloway: *Um, very many, so many.*

Ziwe: *Very many?*[9]

I just had the strangest interaction. I was hiking along a dirt road, searching for the will to write. It was the same path my friends and I had walked for weeks. But this time, I was alone, with no one aware of where I was.

I was not initially afraid when I saw a white Subaru approaching in the distance. I took a step off the dirt road to make way for the midsize sedan. I smiled, hoping that would be the extent of our interaction. But the car stopped and the driver rolled down his window.

This made me nervous. I was used to the talkative locals—a week prior, three separate yet equally exasperated census workers chatted with me hoping to get a head count on the town's citizenry. But this time felt different.

---

9   Excerpt from interview with Caroline Calloway, June 18, 2020, on Instagram Live.

A smiling brown-haired man with a Supercuts haircut peered out of his car. "What are you doing here?" he said.

I did not respond because I could have asked him the same thing. I had explored this trail enough to know it led in the opposite direction of town. Nothing was there other than woods . . . and more woods.

I was alone, standing one foot away from a road barely wide enough to fit the car famous for its socially progressive drivers. I had about as much business being there as he did; we were in a place where deer outnumbered people and ticks outnumbered deer.

"Who are you?"

Again, I did not respond.

His tone indicated that he was not going to leave me alone until I said something. Anything. Today, he had elected himself as sheriff of the woods, and his sole duty was to make sure that I did not damage any twigs. It didn't matter that I was a young woman. It didn't matter that I was wearing a comically large faux-fur hat in the middle of the summer. Or that I was toting around a lilac-colored children's backpack. Or that we were living through a global pandemic that encouraged limited interactions with strangers. No, as sworn protector of the woodlands, it was this man's job to make sure I was conducting myself appropriately.

Toni Morrison once said that racism was a distraction. It keeps you explaining, over and over again, your reason for being, wasting your time proving to others what you know to be true.

I was walking through the woods in the middle of the day because I had writer's block. (Which was none of his business.) It had taken so much effort to get to a place in my professional life where I could afford to rent a cabin on my own (which was also none of his business), and here I was having to justify my right to enjoy the same woods as some random dude driving a car for lesbians. Somehow, I found myself accountable to a man I had never met. But the caveat was that in this trigger-happy environment, if I did not waste my time on an explanation, this misunderstanding could be my last.

I just stared at him in my indignant way that over the past year had prompted rambling, nervous confessions from interview guests on Instagram Live. He stared back at me. But this time I was not asking, "How many black friends do you have?" Instead, I was doing Jason Bourne calculations on whether I could outrun this strange man in these densely packed woods. When, exactly, would be the right moment to start sprinting?

Once more: "Why are you here?"

When I am afraid, I listen. It was noon. The songbirds cooed. The leaves rustled in the wind. But it was my silence that filled the valley.

"Are you staying in the Airbnb? We own this property."

That is when I noticed that the brunette man was sitting beside a blonde woman. She had not moved, so it was hard to tell if she was his victim or accomplice.

I spoke in a tone several octaves higher than my speaking voice. A skill that I picked up in private school to assuage the fear that my appearance stoked.

"Thank you for letting me stay at your place, I love your home. You live at [REDACTED]?"

"No, we do not live there, we're just neighbors. So you *are* staying at the Airbnb?"

That was the moment my heart started beating. He didn't own the rental. He was guarding property that didn't even belong to him. I could not trust another word that came out of this man's mouth. I caught him in a lie.

At that moment I was afraid this white man was going to murder me.

Or abduct me.

Or rape me.

Or abduct me and *then* rape me and then murder me.

I knew I would not be the first woman to go missing in these woods. The woods were full of apparitions, as the land formerly settled by the Lenape Confederation[10] and now a short-term rental destabilizing the housing market for $400 a night.

---

10   I was recently at a live alternative-comedy show in Brooklyn where the host opened the show with a land acknowledgment, which is a statement that recognizes Indigenous peoples'

"What is your name?"

I considered how quickly Subarus could reverse. It probably had four-wheel drive, which means nothing to me because this was the middle of the summer and I do not know what four-wheel drive is. If I was going to run, it would be uphill through the thicket to another desolate road. The nearest house was probably two miles away, and its lawn was decorated with signs that pledged to Make America Great Again. Years of coming in last place at cross-country meets had taught me that I was a horrible distance runner but above average at sprinting. I began shifting the weight on my feet.

"You do know that you are trespassing. The property you're staying on is on this side of the road, and the side of the road you're standing on belongs to Eliot Spitzer."

I knew that this was a famous old white man, but I could not place exactly who he was or why I knew his name. A cursory google hours later would tell me this was the former governor of New York who resigned in disgrace after a scandal involving sex workers. If I stumbled upon Eliot Spitzer alone in the woods, I think I'd have more cause for concern than he would.

---

history on the land rather than erasing their culture. The host held a moment of silence and I thought about how the performers and audience were occupying territory that belonged to the Lenape. While I am marginalized in my own right, it is important to acknowledge my complicity in the occupation of stolen land. Whenever I go upstate, I think about how the woods interconnected from southeastern New York and northeastern New Jersey to Delaware and parts of Pennsylvania, Maryland, and Virginia belonged to neither me nor the strange man but the Indigenous peoples who came before us. Immediately after the moment of silence, I watched three guys named Matt play a round of Zip, Zap, Zop.

"You have to understand that what you're doing is a little bit strange."

Mind you, what I was "doing" was "walking in the woods" in a "black top hat." I was not committing an illegal act; I was one foot away from the public road, and we were on three hundred acres of secluded forest. The only person who cared, the only person who knew I was there, was this man who made it his civic duty to make sure I did not steal the woods (?!). I am not sure what he was afraid of, but as is usually the case, his fear was now my black-ass problem.

"You have to understand during this political climate why I would not want to talk to a white guy in the woods," I defended. My words surprised the man as much as I surprised myself. I had said the quiet part out loud. And then came the hemming and hawing.

"Oh, we totally get it! My name is Justin. And this is my wife, Blah Blah Blah." The blonde lady smiled. I immediately forgot her name. I remember it being Karen, but it was definitely not Karen ... or was it? Justin, however, was not a name I could forget. I had gone to school with a couple of Justins, many of whom were emotional terrorists.[11]

"She didn't know, honey. It's okay," Karen insisted. I couldn't appreciate her protests. She had watched her partner interrogate me and didn't have any objections until I spoke up for myself.

---

11 No disrespect to any Justins reading my book. I realize that being prejudiced against names is ignorant. Please allow me patience and grace to unlearn my biases and become a better ally to the Justin community.

By August 2020, activism, or the performance of it, had become all the rage. As a society, we had collectively discovered that racism was bad. While it's troubling to consider the implications of this "movement"—perhaps society was okay with racism until now (??)—and if anti-racism is a trend, the nature of cycles suggests it will eventually fall out of trend (?!). I was left with a modicum of hope that in real time turned to skepticism. I could tell by Karen's protests that she knew why confronting me was weird but she could not convince her husband. I bet they would've voted for Obama for a third term.

I could not offer the couple anything other than my silence. She tried to console me.

"Don't worry about us, we have a black friend in the back."

All I could see was my black face looking back at me from their tinted car windows. I wondered if I was the "black friend" this couple was going to enjoy for their weird little Jordan Peele fantasy.

"What is your name?"

I had pepper spray in the front pocket of my mini backpack. I could reach it without taking off my bag. But putting my arms behind my back would spook this coexist couple. Running was my only option, but how many more people were in the back of that sedan with tinted windows? From where I was standing, the only ally I had was my reflection, the only black friend for miles.

My next move had to be intentional.

"Well, hi, I would say hi to your black friend, but I cannot see them."

I have made a career out of blending a tone between sarcastic and earnest. It is hard for strangers to tell what I am thinking. Sometimes, it is hard for me to tell what I am thinking.

The couple argued, whispering among themselves for far too long.

Slowly, the back window lowered and an emaciated black child appeared behind my reflection. Their black friend was what I could only assume was their black adopted daughter. She looked like me as a child, except her eyes were so wide they looked sewn open.

"Hi!" This was the first time I had spoken with any affectation other than visceral disdain. My friendliness toward the black child subdued her white guardians.

But their little black friend did not say anything back to me. She just stared with those large porcelain eyes. I wondered who needed saving: me, her, or both of us.

"She likes to go swimming at the house you're staying at," Karen coaxed. But the child's silence filled the sunken place.

"I love swimming," I offered. "It is too cold, so I haven't been able to do it as much as I wanted, though."

"It is too cold . . ." Karen and Justin repeated to each other as if they were learning for the first time that I shared their language.

The black friend held my eye contact, and, without warning, fury possessed the little girl and she screamed, "LUCKY!!!!!!!"

Her voice was both shrill and deep like an incantation. It was hard to believe that in this conversation, I was the lucky one.

"Okay . . ." I concluded, looking at the parents. I was done speaking.

"Next time, just know that you're supposed to be on the other side of the road."

"Okay."

"That side is Eliot's."

"Okay."

"She did not know, Justin."

"Okay."

"Have a good day."

"Okay."

And then they drove off with the window down. The black friend that they had used to assuage their racial guilt, the black friend to quell my fears about their interrogation, did not break eye contact with me. We looked at each other until the car reached the top of the hill. I worried for her safety and she envied mine. I was lucky. So often, I hear people refer to nameless, faceless black friends who function more as symbolic proof of tolerance rather than as actual people.

Sure, I wore blackface, but some of my best friends are black.

Sure, I touched your hair, but some of my best friends are black.

Sure, I stopped you while hiking alone in the woods, but some of my best friends are black and one is also in this car.

However, she was not a black friend. She was a child who wanted to be anywhere but that Subaru. I knew exactly where she was coming from, because I had spent the past five minutes fearing their friendship too.

Weeks later I left a review for the Airbnb host and mentioned the incident. The owner apologized and told me he had never heard of Justin.

wikifeet

Ziwe: What's the racial demographic of your fans on OnlyFans?

Mia Khalifa: Latin, mostly.

Ziwe: Really?!

Mia Khalifa: Yeah.

Ziwe: Okay, shout out. Do they have favorite body parts, like elbow versus back-knee versus—

Mia Khalifa: Do you want to hear the craziest thing?

Ziwe: What? Wait what?

Mia Khalifa: My feet in socks. Or my armpits.

Ziwe: Really?

Mia Khalifa: Yes.

Ziwe: How much money do you think I could get for my black little toes?

Mia Khalifa: I will pay you a thousand dollars for the pinky toe right now.

Ziwe: Well, but you do not know—I am rated "okay" on wikiFeet.

Mia Khalifa: Yeah, no, no, that is racism at its finest. This whole episode, our feet should be censored.

Ziwe: If my foot is not censored, where's the wide? [to the camera operator] If our feet are not censored, someone's getting fired.[12]

Unfortunately, I am on wikiFeet.

For those who do not know, wikiFeet is a photo-sharing foot fetish site dedicated to photos of celebrities' feet. I first noticed that I had been added in 2019, at a time when I would not have described myself as a celebrity. A friend forwarded my rating to me, insisting that I had "made it." The idea that anyone would invest time and energy into ogling my feet was beyond my comprehension, but I was featured on a website that averaged more than three million visitors a month.

I do not judge members of the wikiFeet community. I learned on Tumblr that shaming someone's sexual preferences is problematic (unless of course that sexual preference is illegal). But, personally, *my* sexual preference is that no one looks at my feet ever. I certainly do not want my feet online. Yet, to my horror, I learned that I had a wikiFeet rating of two stars,[13] categorized as "okay feet." While "okay" is technically not an insult, it is not a compliment either. I hate my feet. And also I hate everyone else's feet. In my humble opinion, feet are just ugly hands, and hands are not that cute to

---

12   Excerpt from interview in *ZIWE* S2 E5, "Empowerment with Mia Khalifa," May 29, 2022, on Showtime.

13   Free idea! Rather than rate on a scale of stars, wikiFeet should rate on a scale of toes. There are so many missed opportunities on this website for the puns that foot fetishes provide. The jokes are a shoe-in . . . . See!

begin with. It's fine for me to have disdain for my body's extremities, but for strangers to rate my ten toes as anything other than "perfect," "beautiful," or possibly "dainty" is a racist hate crime that should be punished to the fullest extent of the law. This may seem like an irrational reaction, but you are wrong and stupid and also, shut up!

I am very self-conscious about the way that I look, in part because I am a woman who also happens to be conscious. Since birth, every commercial, every magazine, every piece of media I have encountered has socialized me to hate every body part.

I was an ugly duckling. My hair, which my mother insisted that I chemically straighten, was dry and brittle. Every six to eight weeks, she would slather my head in Just for Me No-Lye Conditioning Crème Relaxer that burned my scalp. Where my natural hair would leave combs broken[14] in its wake, my relaxed hair would break if a breeze hit it wrong. Worst of all, my hair looked nothing like the beaming child on the box, who was selling me an elixir of lies![15] Instead, my hair just became too flat and delicate to support hats, which would have been the best remedy for my shame.

I had severe eczema. The skin above my upper lip had darkened with scarring from a bad habit of nervously licking my lips. I looked like I had a Steve Harvey mustache that was impossible to shave.

---

14   There is a reason Lil Wayne rapped "tougher than Nigerian hair" in his smash hit "A Milli."

15   I recently learned via a Twitter trending topic that all the kids on the Just for Me Crème Relaxer box did not even use the product! They all had natural hair and silky pressed it for shoot days. I believe those of us who were deceived by their bountiful locks are entitled to financial compensation, because there is no way that that acid did not wreak havoc on our synapses.

The rings around my eyes were also discolored. Years later, this discoloration would make it look like I always had on a wispy eye shadow, but at twelve years old, I resembled King Julien, the lemur in *Madagascar.*

I had body odor. As an adult, I am known for smelling fresh like a tropical beach after a rainstorm, because I surround myself with candles and fragrances. However, when I was a child, I was unfamiliar with the concept of deodorant. For some reason that had never been explained to me. Not to point any fingers, but my mother refused to buy me products that acknowledged I had hit puberty. Instead, she would waft her nose and tell me to scrub my armpits harder. The nice thing about smelling horrible is that as the guilty party, you are sort of blissfully unaware. There is a freedom in being smelly and clueless. As the stinky middle-schooler, the difficulty is that people will remark on your rancid scent. The most memorable conversation about my stinkiness was when my sixth-grade teacher, Mr. [REDACTED], pulled me aside during gym class to ask me if my parents were dead. Confused, but always cheery, I informed him that they were not. He was very relieved for me: "Well then tell your mother to buy you deodorant."

In Mr. [REDACTED]'s reality, the only logical explanation for my body odor was that I was an orphan[16] whose parents had died in some freak accident that led to my subsequent neglect in a foster home (???). Not sure I would interrogate an eleven-year-old with such direct questioning about emotional trauma, but public schools are underfunded and you get what you pay for. Months

---

16 Like Oliver Twist!

later, I would repay my debt to Mr. [REDACTED] by consistently reminding the class that he owed us a pizza party.[17]

I had other insecurities. For example, my clothes. When my mother was not trying to put me in traditional *geles*, Nigerian headwraps, I wore high-water pants from Marshalls and unlicensed graphic tees where the Not Disney characters were just slightly off (e.g., *101 Dalmatians* sweatshirts where the dogs were missing their signature spots). When Nelly's "Air Force Ones" dominated the Billboard charts, I did not have designer shoes, instead rocking orthopedic shoes. And I always wore granny panties that hiked far above my waist, despite Manny Santos from *Degrassi: The Next Generation* empowering a generation of young millennials to wear thongs. All of this resulted in my classmates laughing at me, which, thanks to what my therapist describes as habitual disassociation, I did not process in real time.

None of these things were as difficult as being one of the only dark-skinned kids in my class from kindergarten through high school. Before I became familiar with the liberal racism that would go on to influence my work, I learned that even marginalized people have a hierarchy of class and color. When I was in public school, I was one of the only dark people among a sea of fair-skinned Puerto Ricans, Dominicans, and Colombians. This would lead to ridicule, as children are both unimaginative and astonishingly rude. One time in the fifth grade, for instance, Mrs. [REDACTED] prompted

---

17 Mr. [REDACTED] made the mistake of promising a roomful of students that if they had perfect attendance for a week, he'd give us a pizza party. He assumed that we would not be up to the task, which we were, and that we would forget about the promise, which I did not. It actually took months to bully him into fulfilling his promise, which as an adult I now realize is because he could not afford pizza as an underpaid teacher. Whoopsies, my bad!

me to do a presentation on "my perspective." I performed a comedy routine in which I repeated in excruciating detail all of the "festive" nicknames I had in class, like "darkie" and "Africa." After my tight five minutes of stand-up, which I absolutely slayed, my teacher quieted the class and said, "That is sad." She then quickly changed the subject, never acknowledging this "perspective" again. This is a theme in my life. I share a funny story, only for my audience to emphatically warn me to never repeat that story again.[18] I would judge my teacher for a lack of follow-up on what was clearly harassment protected under the Bill of Rights, but she was a pregnant public school teacher, and we were lucky we had school supplies. Things did not get better with time. When I was in private school, I was one of few black kids in an ocean of Kennedy-esque blondes and brunettes with inherited wealth. I would not describe either period as a great place for me to come into my self-confidence as a beautiful young black woman.

I thought I was ugly for a very long time, and now, lucky for me, strangers ranked my insecurities online. I found myself on wikiFeet—against my will, I might add—in the form of a photo of me from college, on a Lake Michigan beach in a peach bikini from Forever 21. I remember posing for the photo and purposefully burying my toes in the sand to conceal them. I was not hiding my feet from the world; I was hiding the world from my feet. But my fatal mistake was that this was the one photo on social media in which I had not cropped out my feet entirely.

---

18   Here's a funny story that is actually sad. To celebrate Grandparents' Day, my second-grade teacher, Mrs. [REDACTED], insisted that her students draw things that we liked to do with our grandparents. All of my grandparents are dead, information that I politely relayed to my teacher, only for her to insist that I draw an image of what I would do with my grandparents if they were still alive. I drew a picture of four angels pushing me on a swing. I find this hilarious. But it is a story friends tell me not to repeat because it is also sad . . . and now it's in print forever!

I had photoshopped the thirst trap to include book covers of *Animal Farm*, *The New Jim Crow*, *The Feminine Mystique*, and *Twelve Years a Slave*, arranged intentionally to cover everything but my youthful, bountiful breasts as a parody of a then-viral photo of Matt McGorry[19] shirtless in glasses reading *The New Jim Crow*. I captioned the photograph thusly: "'The New Jim Crow' by #MichelleAlexander is absolutely brilliant. Pls read full post."

For years, I had been so careful to not let anything below my ankles be exposed for the internet to see, but the source of my demise was a hilariously dank meme. No one's fault but my own—the lesson here is that no cruel deed goes unpunished.[20]

WikiFeet is one of the most innocuous demonstrations of the pros and cons of being a famous woman. The pros of course are celebrity, fortune, and an unlimited supply of fedoras that you could only ever dream of. The con is a total invasion of privacy where strangers rank your body parts on a message board.

Britney Spears, the defining celebrity of my childhood, is also on wikiFeet. My friends interpreted this benchmark as a reflection of my expansive fame and influence. On the surface, this seems like good company in which to find myself. I knew the words to every song and the moves to every dance, and I could quote every interview. When Britney debuted "*Oops!... I Did It Again*" on Nickelodeon, I held my rainbow-colored Fisher-Price tape recorder to the TV and recorded that performance, telling my family to shut the fuck

---

19   Note: While writing this essay, I had forgotten what Matt's last name was, so I just googled "Matt Woke" and found him and the selfie. That is called good branding! Matt Woke wins.

20   I also learned that God apparently loves Matt McGorry. Good for him.

up until Britney finished her performance. I wore that recording *out* until the tape disintegrated.[21] In fact, the single greatest resentment that I am harboring as an adult is that *someone* threw away my Britney Spears Scholastic book that I bought by collecting pennies from in between couch cushions, because as a religious person she would not finance such a secular investment.[22] *Someone* felt as though Britney Spears was not a good example, even though Britney Spears was one of the few things that made me happy.

Growing up, all I wanted was to be as confident as Britney Spears, as sexy as Britney Spears, and as desired as Britney Spears. Where I was an ugly outcast with crooked teeth and a halo of stench surrounding me that rivaled Charlie Brown's friend Pig-Pen, my queen Britney Jean Spears was the princess of pop music.[23] It was not until years later that I learned one of my greatest influences had been placed under an oppressive conservatorship[24] that allegedly

---

21   Cassette tapes wearing down until the tape ripped is something that used to happen in the '90s. Children today will never appreciate how good they have it just streaming ten thousand songs from the cloud with no concern for memory space as their favorite artists do not get compensated. Younger generations will also never know what it is like to not have acid rain from the sky as wildfires ravage California, so I guess it is a trade-off.

22   My mother did not tell me she threw it away; one day it just went missing, and when I asked her where it went, she suggested that I probably misplaced it. I tore our apartment up and down looking for my favorite book, but I never found it.

23   Years later, a very kind reporter, Kasia, would insist on describing me as the princess of pop in a listing of my monthly comedy show, *Pop Show*, but the *New York Times* fact-checking department would not budge. Instead, I was characterized as someone who "may not be the princess of pop," which . . . is not the same . . . In fact, it is the *exact* opposite.

24   When I, like so many, watched the *New York Times* Britney Spears documentary *Framing Britney Spears*, I was transported back to my early teens, when Britney was a punchline for tabloids and late-night shows every night. Britney Spears was placed under conservatorship at age twenty-six, subjected to the supervision of her father, who, according to this documentary, allegedly had little involvement in her early life. Not only is it patriarchal to place a woman's life under the guidance of the nearest man, regardless of their relationship and his skill set; it is also illogical. Was the plan to keep Britney under conservatorship from age twenty-six until death? How could someone be mentally sound enough to work but not sound enough to enjoy the compensation they received for their work? How is this legal? Years later, I found myself at Elsewhere in Bushwick sobbing during Pride weekend, as Britney Spears's "Get Naked" played from the speakers. This was mere days after her bombshell testimony about the abuse

forced her to perform against her will, *allegedly* disallowed her from removing her birth control so she could get pregnant, and *allegedly* medicated her with lithium against her will. What does it say about a society when one of its most famous women is held captive in plain sight as a result of our collective objectification and dehumanization?

The more I examine Britney Spears, the more our wikiFeet commonality feels less like a bastion of honor and more like an insidious tax on womanhood. Britney Spears, who has more than 3,600 total votes with an overall four-star ranking of "nice feet," gets a bunch of impassioned comments.

One comment said,

> *one of the most beautiful picks I've seen lately made me realize how much I miss Britney. If it wasn't for that chair, this pick would be perfect.*

Another comment said,

> *I hate that frigging chair with every fiber of my being. Fate decided to screw us over by ruining what could have been the best outdoor sole shots of Britney in the hot sun for all of us to enjoy. What a shame. It's an absolute tragedy.*

---

she had experienced at the hands of her father with no immediate change in the status of her autonomy. Listening to the voice of a woman who seemed to belong to everyone but herself reminded me of her strength, because even as Britney suffered in isolation, her words moved millions—excuse me, billions—to dance. She reminds me that there are some souls that you cannot keep down. Some people are destined to be great. Britney Spears has given us so much, and she deserves a life free of harassment. And just as importantly, she shed light on the bias in conservatorships that make those the state deems mentally ill forfeit their rights. Free Britney! Free all who are unjustly imprisoned!

A third user said,

> *Feet abuse, three stars.*

The people were upset at the chair for blocking the creep shot of Britney's feet. It was all a lot to process, but one comment stuck out to me:

> *I keep seeing comments on other pages that say she had ugly feet. They are not Victoria Justice level but they are not ugly. [4/4/17 at 6:04 p.m.]*

Now, why do we have to compare women's feet at all? Britney has her lane and Victoria has her lane and there is still space for both of these women's feet. But naturally, I had to research what was so good about Victoria Justice's feet. Which I was shocked to learn is . . . everything? Victoria Justice, formerly of Nickelodeon's *Victorious*, has more than seven thousand votes, with a rare five-star rating that averages "gorgeous feet." Not only does Ms. Justice have better, smaller feet than me, but according to this wiki she is also younger.

Her comments were much hornier, especially on a photo of her stomping grapes:

> *Holy crap. I so want the win that is made from these grapes. I would drink the win, oh sorry, drink the win that Victoria helped make with her sexy feet crushing those grapes.*

These people were so dizzy with lust that they couldn't spell "wine" correctly.

Meanwhile, I had one kind but sparing comment that just said "Nice feet girl" [6/27/2020 at 12:22 P.M.] at the height of a global pandemic. It gives me solace knowing that my sand-covered corns provide some sweet soul enough comfort to prompt a kind word in return. Still, I couldn't forget that my feet were ranked "okay" by a whopping five people. One vote for "beautiful," one vote for "nice," two votes for "okay," and then one hater who voted "ugly." I am not sure that the wikiFeet community realizes that by reducing women to just feet scores, they are dehumanizing us. But intention is not an excuse for impact. I am more than ten toes and eerily flat feet. I also have a beautiful heart under two moderately sized breasts.[25] Thus, I am demanding a call to action. Please go to wikifeet.com, create a user account on this collaborative celebrity feet database, and vote for me like my self-confidence depends on it.

I am ashamed to admit that I still care what people think about my feet. I care what people think about me. These insecurities make me human. The best lesson I ever internalized is that no one will love me, or my feet, like I love myself. Imperfectly perfect. I learned this from an episode of *Sailor Moon*. This is a difficult task, as I am constantly reminding myself that I deserve patience and generosity and warmth.[26] However, the key to life is to approach this practice one step at a time. One day everyone and everything we

---

25 For now! Call me, Dr. Miami?

26 And compliments on my feet, which I should note are getting better by the day thanks to extreme procedures like feet chemical peels.

know will turn to dust, except plastic, which will take at least 450 years to biodegrade. In the meantime, I will enjoy every part of me and my sole.[27] So what if my feet do not compare to Victoria Justice's? They allow me the freedom to dance to Britney Spears with my friends. And for that, I am grateful.

---

27 Pun intended, boom!

discomfort

Ziwe: What advice would you give my Nigerian parents?

Julio Torres: When—how old were they when they came?

Ziwe: No, I just mean, just like, today. In 2021. They are Nigerian, um—

Julio Torres: Ho—What do they need advice in?

Ziwe: Um, I do not know!

Julio Torres: Um . . . uh . . .

Ziwe: Being African? Living in the United States? Having a daughter that is both gorgeous and emotionally unavailable?

Julio Torres: Um, I would say uh—keep . . . doing, what you've been doing with Ziwe, 'cause look at her now, she has a show.

Ziwe: That is really, really weird that you would talk to my parents like that. No respect.

Julio Torres: No-no-no, reverence.

Ziwe: My culture's different from your culture, you have to give your elders proper due.

Julio Torres: Um, how—how do they like to be addressed?

Ziwe: Um, not at all.

Julio Torres: Not at all?

Ziwe: No . . . do not talk to them.

Julio Torres: Okay, then I would not.[28]

Some of you have never had to be the only person in a friend group to miss a sleepover because your immigrant parents didn't trust other people, and it shows. Culturally, sleepovers are not something that I am familiar with. But television has a way of indoctrinating children into a belief system of what constitutes "normal" where any sort of outlier from the televised norm is seen as exactly that—an outlier—even if there are billions of people who do not reflect the world presented on the screen. I grew up watching reruns of *Growing Pains, Full House, Smart Guy,* and *Sister, Sister.* I so desperately wanted to have a family life that reflected those picture-perfect fantasies.

As a child, occasionally, I would press my mother about why I couldn't live out my Mary-Kate and Ashley dreams, pulling all-nighters with my friends. She told me that sleeping on the floor was the reason they left Nigeria. My parents also gave this reason when I asked them if we would ever go camping: *Why would we sleep outside? That's why we left Nigeria.* I thought my parents' logic was unfair. They thought I was ungrateful. If I was lucky enough to have my own bed, why did I not want to sleep in it? There were plenty of children out there who did not have houses to call home.

---

28 Excerpt from interview in *ZIWE* S1 E5, "Immigration with Julio Torres," June 6, 2021, on Showtime.

My parents are Nigerian immigrants—Igbo and Ijaw. The best way to describe their culture is a sort of terse, tough love. They were raised with a set of rules that I too learned by trial and error.

Some rules were innocuous. Like the fact that there is a fundamental difference between outside clothes and inside clothes. Outside clothes, you wear outside—to run errands, to take out the trash, to get coffee, etc. Indoor clothes, you wear in the house—to lounge, lie in bed, etc.[29] The only times you wear your outside clothes indoors are (1) to put them on, (2) to take them off, and (3) because you have a guest coming over. The one thing that you do not do under any circumstances is wear your outside clothes in bed. That is the most disgusting, heinous, vile sin that one could commit in a Nigerian household. I have lived away from home since I was fourteen years old, and the biggest cultural shock to me is seeing people wear the clothes in which they spent the entire day getting dirty in the same place that they sleep. Not only is this unsanitary, but it is the leading cause of disease, according to me, a first-generation immigrant. Do not do that.[30]

Other rules adhered to their own biases and were not by today's American standards[31] considered politically correct. The most

---

29 Athleisure brands that blend lounging with activity would be incomprehensible to them.

30 Also, do not put your suitcase on your bed. Your suitcase has been flung and dragged and kicked halfway around the country with no discernment for the pools of muck that it comes into contact with. Do not put that on your bed. And this should go without saying, but also do not put your shoes on your bed. Despite what sitcoms suggest, it is not even comfortable to wear a kitten heel on a padded mattress. It is inappropriate to wear shoes around the house at all. God invented slippers for a reason. Shoes belong outside because they are covered in outside juice. Stop being nasty and take off your shoes.

31 The thing about standards is that they are all relative to people's culture. I was listening to an episode of *Freakonomics* that described American culture as different from other cultures. To some this may be an astute observation, but to anyone raised by non-Americans, it is as obvious as two children in a trench coat trying to enter a bar. One example the podcast used

defining lessons of my childhood can be chalked up to my parents having a very gendered way of looking at the world. Fun fact: I am a woman. So, in their cultural hierarchy of success, I am already operating at a deficit. I learned that women were supposed to wear dresses, cook and/or clean, and allow "men to be men," a vague statement that can be interpreted by a child as absolute freedom, and by an adult woman as an unchecked reign of terror. As a result of this culturally conservative upbringing, I was a tomboy. I did not care for the sugar, spice, and everything nice that girls were supposed to invest in. I preferred ESPN and *American Psycho* and *Grand Theft Auto: San Andreas*. I identified with the butch Powerpuff Girl, Buttercup,[32] because she wasn't afraid to get her fingerless hands dirty.

I realized at a very young age that being a boy rules and being a girl drools. Boys get to play outside and stay out late and swear. Much to my parents' chagrin, I (a girl!) refused to wear dresses, I never cleaned, and I spent as little time in the kitchen as possible.[33] This meant that I could not carry on the cultural traditions of cooking Nigerian food like jollof rice and fufu. I saw my conscientious objection to all practical life skills as a protest against the misog-

---

was the tourist Michael Fay, who was sentenced to four months in jail and six strokes of caning after stealing road signs and vandalizing eighteen cars in Singapore. President Bill Clinton described the punishment as "extreme," pressuring the Singaporean government to grant Fay clemency. Singapore stood its ground, noting that this punishment was a normal part of their legal system. On May 5, 1994, despite international outcries, Michael Fay, who had his sentence reduced, was struck four times on his butt with a rattan cane as he cried out "I'm dying," according to reporting by Reuters and the *New York Times*. To many Americans, this is not normal. To me, this is just a spanking. Normal is relative.

32   I believe Buttercup, as a queer icon, deserves a GLAAD Award.

33   This rebellion is an issue for me, because I do not cook enough. I would never say that I cannot cook. I can follow simple instructions, therefore I can cook. But the nuances of mixing and matching ingredients by citrus are lost on me. Think of all the tasty foods I would treat myself to had I not also survived the prison of my gender.

yny that was trying to oppress me. There comes a time in every person's life where they must take a stand against tyranny and do the right thing. In this case, "tyranny" was the woman who gave birth to me, and "the right thing" was not taking care of myself. Even at eight years old, I wondered what was so essential about a young girl learning how to tend to her home. Sexism! Misogyny! I was just old enough to know I was getting played by the system, especially as I saw boys my age gallivant freely as I suffered through household tasks like Little Orphan Annie.[34]

Instead, I would suppress myself. After all, boys ate food and lived in homes and needed clean underwear just as much as girls did. If they weren't going to be forced to learn how to do these things, neither was I.

Worshipping "manly things" gave me what I thought was power over the limitations of my femininity. In actuality, it reinforced my sexist oppression. My logic was that I was not like other girls because I was a girl who liked boy things because boy things were inherently better. But boy things and girl things are not immutable facts; they are a construct. During the 1700s, French noblemen wore heels to signal their aristocracy. Now heels represent the beauty labor that women have to do to appear attractive and appeal to the male gaze. Whereas men are not usually expected to put on makeup, do their hair, or wear fashionable clothes, women must put in this effort to be seen as valuable in their femininity. Normal is not a fixed point in history. And in pushing arbitrary gender roles on me, my parents had fueled my adolescent rebellion against my gender.

---

34   Obviously, I am referring to the Quvenzhané Wallis version of Annie, because representation in orphans matters.

This is something I tried to explain to my parents. They did not love it. I cannot say for sure whether they were worried that my boyish behavior would make me a lesbian, but they kindly suggested on more than one occasion that I should stop wearing purple because people would think I was gay.[35] With this policing, I had a distinct understanding of what it meant to be a woman in the world: It was *mid* at best. No power. No credit. No rights. Just a lot of people being mad at you for not being perfect when perfection was a moving goalpost. I was just supposed to accept that that was the way the world operated. My performance of gender, or lack thereof, meant that there was always a part of my parents' approval I would not be able to attain. This is most evident in my work.

My mother is not going to read this book. She did not watch my show. She does not engage in any number of creative endeavors I have had over the course of my career. My work is not something that we discuss. It is not that she doesn't care; it is that she believes my work is secular.

I have made a conscious effort to ask my mother more questions as she gets older. I am more afraid to ask her questions than anything I've ever asked my interview subjects. Today, I texted her to ask what it was like seeing snow for the first time. My mother answered and then promptly texted me saying, "Please be careful about who you divulge my personal information to." Privacy is a Nigerian value.

We do not discuss much aside from food and God. There are many reasons why, but the most obvious is that we are two differ-

---

35   The color of gay (?!).

ent women from two different cultures with two different styles of communicating. Our relationship is not normal to me. I long for the picture-perfect relationship seen in *Full House* where after thirty minutes of hijinks, Michelle Tanner hugs her dad, Danny, and the audience coos. As a child you wonder: Why don't my parents have normal rules? Why don't we eat normal food? Why don't we wear normal clothes? Why can't we just be normal?

My upbringing was out of my control. It's hard to accept. I am not someone who accepts that there are things that are "out of my control." I am the dangerous combination of Nigerian and New Englander, which means that I can repress emotions before I even register the act of *feeling*. It also means that I hate to talk about myself. Which, by the transitive property, means that I hate being on the receiving end of interviews.

Most interviews start out with the interviewer telling me that they are afraid of me. Now, intellectuals may notice that "I am afraid to talk to you" is not technically a question, and to that observation, I simply say, yes! After these interviewers compliment me, they usually ask me two questions:

1. They ask me how I am able to ask uncomfortable questions without feeling uncomfortable.

2. They ask me if my parents are proud of me.

I find the latter infantilizing. I hate when interviewers ask me about my parents. I do not want people to know anything about me. I do not want people to know if I am married. I do not want people to know if I have children. I do not want people to take photos of the back of my head as I meander around Alphabet City because the streets confuse me and I'm afraid of rats. I prefer to be an enigma. I do not want my personal information divulged. Remember, *privacy is a Nigerian value.*

However, entertainment is an industry where the personal bleeds into the professional.[36] For audiences to feel like they can relate to you, they must "know" "you." It doesn't matter that you are here to promote your show/book/album/Arthur George sock line; you must share fun tidbits about the most formative relationships you've ever had. An unforgettable example of this was Barbara Walters's[37] 2000 ABC interview with Ricky Martin.

---

36 I am a celebrity-rights activist. I do not believe the public is entitled to know anything about celebrities other than the release date of their work and their favorite projects to do. And this is not because I herald celebrities as superhumans deserving of special treatment. Quite the opposite. I don't think much of celebrities at all, because really they are just people who are slightly more attractive than the rest of society. My argument isn't that we shouldn't care what sexuality our favorite performers are. That curiosity is inherent in any adulation. My argument is that we should care quietly, not pry, and respect them enough to mind our business and talk shit in our private group chats. Therefore, hitherto, in conclusion, celebrity rights are human rights.

37 Barbara Walters died on December 30, 2022. The best way to summarize her contributions to journalism is to remember her final episode of *The View.* Oprah Winfrey led a parade of female journalists of all ages, races, and political ideologies across multiple networks, including Diane Sawyer, Robin Roberts, Lara Spencer, Elizabeth Vargas, Amy Robach, Juju Chang, Deborah Roberts, Katie Couric, Savannah Guthrie, Natalie Morales, Tamron Hall, Maria Shriver, Cynthia McFadden, Kathie Lee Gifford, Hoda Kotb, Jane Pauley, Gayle King, Gretchen Carlson, Deborah Norville, Paula Zahn, Connie Chung, and Joan Lunden. One woman after the next hugged an overwhelmed Barbara Walters as they honored the icon for her trailblazing career. In 1974, Walters made television history as the first female co-host of NBC's *Today* show. Two years later she moved to ABC to become the first female co-anchor of an evening news show. Her work blended the line between journalism and entertainment, and she was known for extracting sensitive information and even pushing some of her subjects to cry. In an interview with Monica Lewinsky, Barbara asked, "You told friends that at one time or another your mother and your father because of things that were revealed, the most personal thing about them—that each of them considered taking their own lives—it was that bad? They did?" Monica nods and begins to cry. "People have no idea what this has done . . . Behind the name Monica Lewinsky there is a person, and there is a family, and there is so much pain that has been caused by all this." This ABC News interview was one of their most watched in history, drawing 74 million viewers. But Walters was admonished for injecting her views into the story.
Walters: What will you tell your children when you have them?
Lewinsky: Mommy made a big mistake.

I think about this interview every day. Over the course of this exchange, the seasoned broadcast journalist confronted the pop star about his sexuality as he deflected direct questions about whether or not he identified as gay. At the time, he was riding the success of his global hits "Livin' La Vida Loca" and "She Bangs," but Barbara Walters's attempt to drag him out of the closet was enough to derail his meteoric rise. Nearly ten years later, Barbara Walters conceded that her questions were "inappropriate." In this mistake, Walter taught a valuable lesson that we still do not heed. Dragging celebrities out of the closet is not just a product of the early millennium, as to this day the internet constantly speculates about the sexualities of certain pop stars with effeminate voices or affinities for sequins. In any other industry, it would be inappropriate to probe your coworkers about anything other than their work and the information they volunteer.[38] But

---

Walters: And that is the understatement of the year.

Despite Walters's bias, Lewinsky tweeted a tribute to the late journalist: "The very first person with whom i ever sat for a television interview . . . and will certainly be my most memorable. barbara will be missed by many—including me. sending love to jackie, george + her other friends. #RIPBarbara." The young woman who had directly been in the line of her fire had admiration and respect for her work. This is a testament to Barbara Walters's skill but also a testament to the craft of journalism. Barbara Walters never faltered in connecting stories to her subjects' humanity and her own. As public relations professionals now outpace journalists five to one, it is more imperative than ever to appreciate the value of journalists. There is no such thing as an unbiased press, and rather than upholding individuals to impossible standards we must examine their bias in the context of their reporting. A huge part of every story is the media's interpretation of what is normal and what is not. When I was growing up, my father and I read the local *Eagle-Tribune* and watched *ABC World News* every single day at 6:30 P.M. Eastern. At the time, I didn't know that my father's obsession with news was special. He was an adult who was constantly informed, and therefore I was a child who was informed. Those early habits established my love and appreciation of journalists and their commitment to deliver the truth in spite of a hostile culture toward the press and the First Amendment. But more than anything, they are the foundation of my work, as I blend journalism with entertainment for comedy. Journalists, though some may be saints and others may be sinners, are integral to our world.

38   Personally, I am envious of surgeons who I assume clock in (???), suture up organs to get paid $400,000 a year, and then clock out, answering the only questions that interrupt their personal life with "No, that is not a rash" and "Yes, I am a doctor on this flight to Margaritaville."

entertainment makes commodities out of its subjects[39] and their private lives.

Do men get asked if their parents are proud of them? I am not even sure if other women get asked this. It could be because of my youthful glow. As someone who identifies as nineteen, goo goo gah gah, I jokingly project the energy of a child who needs a permission slip to watch scary movies. This is an impossible question to answer without appearing not normal. *Yes, my parents are so proud of me because all their lives they had to fight.* Not only is this true, but it has all the makings of a Cinderella story, which Hollywood loves. But my personal relationships are more complex. All relationships are complex. Impossible questions are the foundation on which my home is built, but in this instance, I do not know what the punch line should be.

I like to think that I do not create art to make my parents proud, but rather to make money.[40] But my art is influenced by my upbringing. As an adult, I get asked if pink is my favorite color because my interview set looked like a Barbie Malibu Dreamhouse. The answer is . . . not exactly. Growing up, I was so bitter and resentful about being a girl that my show became an homage to the cliché of womanhood. My professional obsession with the color pink stems from the performance[41] of femininity I rejected as a

---

39   Actors are our most beautiful laborers. They exist on the precipice of the working and ruling class. But, like most, they sell their labor to the highest bidder. They can get fired. They can get injured. They have a union. It is less likely that an actor makes $20 million per movie and owns a culturally insensitive liquor brand and more likely that they book a national commercial once a year that just barely allows them to afford health care. Did you know the average actor makes about $56,000? In other words, Sydney Sweeney was right! #JeSuisSweeney.

40   Hopefully lots of it! Inshallah!

41   I hate when people refer to what I do as performance art. People only say that about eccentric women who wear organic deodorant and whom they don't know how to describe.

child. The femininity I perform is exactly the daughter my parents tried to raise. It's a hyperfeminine version of a late-night talk show host. The set wasn't just a little pink; it was laughably pink, to the point where in color-correction sessions, my eyes looked bloodshot because there was so much pink refracting off my body. That character upholds the implications of femininity—dressed in sexy outfits, outwardly performing nurture, saying "goo goo gah gah I'm nineteen," infantilizing myself like the harmless girl I was supposed to be. This is drag to me. It codifies the message of the show, the message of individual women who range in thoughts and feelings. It's Barbie packaging, but when you bite into the sandwich, you taste barbed wire.

The truth is, I create art to heal my inner child—the young girl who did not have the words to explain the world herself. I hate when interviewers ask me about my parents, because I do not like to lie. But, when I am honest, people do not respond well! It makes strangers genuinely uncomfortable to ask the question "Are your parents proud of you?" and hear the answer "I do not know." As a self-diagnosed empath, I can feel[42] their disappointment, hoping for a more comforting quote like "Yes, my life is all just an elaborate ruse to get my parents' approval. Yes, Mommy and Daddy are so proud of me. Yes, I am my ancestors' wildest dreams."[43]

Marina Abramović. Björk, Yoko Ono. I am not whimsical. I am not avant-garde. I'm a comedian. I demand to be taken seriously as a clown.

42   And no, I am not a narcissist, I am just a Pisces.

43   I AM my ancestors' wildest dreams. Shout out to them, they died before dial-up internet; they'd be amazed to hear that I spend my days arguing about *Real Housewives* on Reddit.

One time, I was honest and told an interviewer that my mother does not engage with the secular aspects of my life.[44] The interviewer rejected my true statement and then returned to this question several times over the course of a thirty-minute interview, only to end the conversation by saying, "I know in my heart your mother would love your work."[45] Once again, a standard interview had turned into me unpacking the adulthood-formerly-known-as-childhood-trauma of not having normal answers to normal questions because I am not normal.

Fear was the undercurrent I felt when extracting information from my immigrant parents. I did not know how they would react or what innocent question would trigger a lifetime of what I vaguely knew to be bad memories. How many children can relate to the mystery of their parents? My parents are from a different age, or as they would say, *they are not my little friends in the street*. Rather, there is a boundary they establish to maintain respect. It is how they were raised. I know countless first-generation children who can relate to my formal relationship with my parents, who fled war, left their families never to return again, to come to a new country all by themselves with no connections, no money, and no idea what

---

44   My father watches my show because he saw me talking to Gayle King from *CBS This Morning*. He likes my interviews unless he doesn't like them, which he will tell me. Like when he asked why Julia Fox and I were dressed "like that"—I was wearing her signature black raccoon makeup, and Fox had a cut-out top with underboob. One of my family members had to explain to him that it is okay not to like everything about a TV show, advice that he repeated to me without irony.

45   Therapy is a human right. He doesn't know me or my family at all. For all he knows, my mother could be the lady from *A Child Called "It,"* a terrifying memoir I was forced to read in elementary school despite the fact that it gave me, a child, nightmares for weeks because it was *inappropriate* for children. To be clear, this is an analogy; my mother is the opposite of this mentally ill alcoholic antagonist. But the point remains—we do not know anything about the people we see on-screen. We are a culture that watched Chadwick Boseman fight colon cancer for four years right before our eyes and had the nerve to complain about him looking tired and disinterested.

they were supposed to do. Most times, my parents would prefer to never speak about the past. It is not to obscure information from me, it is because remembering is painful. All I have is my ability to piece together family stories I remember hearing (and overhearing) over the course of my life.

Why don't my parents have normal rules? Why don't they eat normal food? Why don't they wear normal clothes? Why can't they just be normal? These questions are xenophobic. It took me a long time to be proud of where I came from. But I am no one without my parents, my Nigerian heritage, my Nigerian ancestors. And by rejecting the lessons that they tried to instill in me, I was literally starving myself of food and, more importantly, of my culture.

For years, my mother pressured me to learn how to make jollof rice.[46] As a kid, I pretended not to pay attention, but jollof rice is one of my favorite dishes to cook. I make it in bulk because I know nothing about proportions, and so I cook for a village even though I'm eating for one.

So, to answer the first question, I am able to ask uncomfortable questions because I have felt uncomfortable my entire life. My mother doesn't need to read my book or watch my show because she is the blueprint. My first friend.

---

46 Nigerian jollof rice is better than Ghanaian jollof rice. There's a war going on between Ghanaians and Nigerians regarding their rice, and Nigerians will be victorious because Nigerians do it better.

how many black friends do you have?

Ziwe: *How many black friends do you have, Alison Roman?*

Alison Roman: *Do you define friend like someone who would pick me up at the airport, or like people I follow or people that I know? Because I have, like, I would say four to five black friends that would pick me up at the airport.*

Ziwe: *Four to five! You are the third person to say they have four to five black friends in the last week to me. Caroline Calloway, Nick Ciarelli, and yourself—*

Alison Roman: *Oh.*

Ziwe: *—that is an interesting statistic.*

Alison Roman: *I actually did not see that part of them. I mean, yeah, I, but that is, like, I know a lot more black people than that that are like friends of mine or friendly, or they are like friends' husbands or wives or partners and people that I know through work, but I mean like actual friends. But like in the grand total of actual friends I have that would pick me up at the airport is probably like twelve to thirteen.*

Ziwe: *Okay, so do your black friends know that you treat them like objects?*

Alison Roman: *[laughs]*[47]

---

47 Excerpt from interview with Alison Roman, June 25, 2020, on Instagram Live.

There is no right answer to the question "How many black friends do you have?" The premise of the question is a trap. As soon as you start to answer, more challenging questions arise. Why do you count your black friends? Do they know that you refer to them as your black friends? Why is the number of black friends you claim so low? Why is it so high? Are these black friends here with us right now? Are you prepared for a FOIA request to verify the validity of these black friendships?

Conversely, if you refuse to answer the question, you come off as suspicious, withholding, even secretive. Do you not have black friends? What do you have to hide? Are you hiding your black friends? Are they safe? Tell the truth!

My truth is that I have never stopped to count all of my friends and sort them by race.[48] That is an odd practice. Which is why I was surprised when several of my interview guests on the weekly Instagram Live show that catapulted my career answered "Four to five" when asked, "How many black friends do you have?"

No more.

No less.

Four to five black friends.

---

48   If anyone were to ask me the racial demographics of my friend group, my answer would be "All of them. Yes! Every. Single. Race. Much like the United States of America, my friends are a melting pot of diverse flavors, like collard greens, queso, and pierogies, which come together to make a very pungent stew. Also, if you assign ethnicities to these three respective dishes, you are part of the problem!"

The first time I heard this answer, it did not strike me as strange. Sure, I considered it a low number of black people to have in one's life, but some people don't have many friends. As I continued to conduct these interviews during the summer of 2020, the coincidence of my guests citing their four to five black friends became a pattern that was hard to ignore, prompting profiles of my show in the *New York Times*,[49] *Vanity Fair*,[50] and *New York* magazine[51] all within the span of two weeks.

Suddenly, one of the biggest questions to come out of my show was not "How many black friends do you have?" but rather,[52] "Why

---

49   "Ziwe Fumudoh Asks: 'How Many Black People Do You Know?,'" by Sandra E. Garcia.

50   "Ziwe Fumudoh Has Mastered the Art of Putting White People on the Spot," by Yohana Desta.

51   "Who's Afraid of Ziwe Fumudoh? For guests who dare to appear on the comedian's Instagram Live show, the question is not if you are racist, but how," by E. Alex Jung.

52   Another question I get asked is "Why would anyone ever agree to do this interview show?" I resent this question. You would be surprised how many people, within one millisecond of meeting me, say "I love your show but you can never interview me." First of all, sir/madam/they/them, you are rude. Second, these shows are premised on consent, both guest and host buying into the chaotic hilarity of being put on the spot, and not looking perfect. It is a modern deconstruction of the American interview, which has devolved from thoughtful discourse about societal issues (Dick Cavett talking to James Baldwin, Muhammad Ali, etc.) to inconsequential conversations about celebrities promoting their movies in between anecdotes of their movies (. . . no examples will be shared, out of respect for the work of my much-more-powerful peers and my career). On the fourth hand, you would never ask this question to Howard Stern, Zach Galifianakis, Andy Cohen, or *The Colbert Report*'s Stephen Colbert—the latter of whom my character is based on—despite the confrontational questions that they've asked their guests for decades. And as for my Fifth Harmony, if you study Oprah Winfrey, the greatest American interviewer in recorded history, you'll recognize that she pioneered the "sensational" interview—which I describe as an interview that is both viral and profound. We want to watch Oprah interview people because she will ask honest questions and get honest answers. In an article in *Salon* titled "Tell Will Smith: 'Ziwe' Will Recoup Your Reputation in Her Barbie Dream House Interrogation Chamber," critic Melanie McFarland explains why a post-slap Will Smith should do my show. McFarland explains, "Adversarial conversations can serve the subject getting grilled, especially if the interviewee understands what the host is up to and is willing to take a few on the chin. And 'Ziwe' is a forum in which the host offers her guests multiple opportunities to apologize for whatever sin they may have committed in the moment, and in a way that amplifies the artificiality of televised atonements . . . Those who do are invariably vindicated not because of what they say but how they present themselves in that act and throughout the rest of the conversation, which almost always includes a ridiculous quiz or a rigged game . . . Any talk show will give the superstar a platform to spout PR-approved bumper-sticker expressions

is saying four to five black friends the default answer for a specific niche of white media liberals?" And just as this question was entering public discourse, the nation was reaching the apex of the Black Lives Matter movement. Catalyzed by the lynching of George Floyd, people across the country (and across the globe) woke up to the idea that racism was not just a tradition of the past but a practice of the present. And while many people were already aware that the premise that "racism exists" and, furthermore, was "something to feel bad about" seemed like an "obvious"[53] "statement," for an even larger group of people, it was a time to self-examine and consider if and how they could be part of the solution of #endingracism.

This racial reckoning resulted in a number of reactions:

- A bunch of racist people getting fired after their underpaid employees "conspired" to do horrible things like "tell the truth" about them.

- Celebrities preemptively admitting they said the n-word[54] even though . . . no one asked.

- Resurfaced photos of public figures in blackface (!!!).

---

like, 'Love is a superpower.' It takes a real one to submit to conversations that rely upon one's sense of humor and sharpness, accepting their believability will not be gauged by what they say but by how they act while saying it."

53   This is said without judgment. A wise woman named Kylie Jenner once said, "This is the year of realizing things." Part of growth is realizing the obvious. As babies realize that fire is hot, we must realize that our purview of the world is not gospel.

54   Celebrities admitting to saying racial slurs was my favorite! If I were not black, I simply would never publicly admit to saying the n-word. I do not care about the guilt; if there is no footage of this bigotry, that is a secret I would take to the grave, after spending the rest of my life atoning for these sins.

I had no idea how popular blackface was until the summer of 2020. Everyone from Canada's sexiest prime minister, [REDACTED], to America's sweetheart [REDACTED] was dabbing their face in Fenty Beauty Pro Filt'r Shade 495[55] and heading to the nearest costume[56] party.

Naturally, when these photos surfaced the refrain was always something along the lines of:

> Oopsies, I did not know I was doing blackface but if I did blackface I am so sorry for the blackface. But I should note this was during a time, four weeks ago, when as a society, we thought blackface was OK. Don't be mad at me, I have black friends!
>
> Much love,
>
> Someone who is sorry they did the Racism™ and/or sorry they got caught publicly doing the Racism™

I've seen this non-apology technique all my life. A celebrity is accused of being racist because they wore blackface or said the n-word or "accidentally" hosted a wedding on a plantation, and their first impulse is to remark on how they could never possibly be racist because they have black friends. This defense is used as if black friends around the world emanate an anti-racist shield

---

55   This would explain why my shade of Fenty is always sold out.

56   Also, I go to one costume party a year and it is Halloween and I basically look like myself except I am scantily clad. Imagine going to a costume party, not during Halloween, and giving a minstrel show?? Goofy! Too much effort! Have they ever heard of a witch hat? They are sold at CVS.

that protects you from doing Racism™ if you stand within a certain radius. The proximity to this black, friendly human shield allows you to unlearn the very foundation of society.

I suppose the idea behind the "Some of my best friends are black" defense is that you cannot be prejudiced if you choose to interact with different racial backgrounds. It suggests that any association with black people is a form of activism when it in fact is the bare minimum of living in a society that includes black people. This kind of friendship seems a bit lopsided: In exchange for proximity to whiteness, a black friend gets the privilege of implicitly (or explicitly) defending all of your friend's racism.

But 2020 marked a change. We are wiser to the fact that having a black friend is not a defense against accusations of racism, just like having a black child does not absolve Thomas Jefferson from being a fugly hater.

In my echo chamber, which I should note is the best echo chamber because I am in it, "Oh, you have a black friend?" became synonymous with "The racist doth protest too much." It's a dog whistle.

In actuality, declaring that you have a black friend after you've done something offensive is like going to a fast-food restaurant, ordering a hot dog, and then remarking on your love of Peppa Pig. Ma'am, this is a Checkers, no one cares, and your love of that rude little piglet will not bring these very smart mammals back to life. Your unprompted diversions have literally nothing to do with the very real accusations.

Many people claim not to have a racist bone in their body. It is of course possible that your femur has never thought of saying the n-word. But when acting together as a unit (read: person), all your bones and tissues and cute little Good Person™ cells might still do something unconsciously. And if your combination of body parts acts together with other units of body parts (read: a group of people), they might accidentally do something together. Suddenly your non-racist bones that were so cute and uniquely yours are nevertheless contributing to upholding a very racist society.

But how many black friends are you supposed to have? When are you allowed to talk about your black friends? Should you just refer to them as friends?

When I ask people, "How many black friends do you have?" I can see in their eyes that they are doing their own sort of approximations. If you answer anything above ten black friends, it is quite obvious to anyone within earshot that you pulled an arbitrary number out of thin air. If you answer anything between six and ten, you look like a weirdo, albeit very popular, who commodifies the brown people in your life. And if you have fewer than three black friends, you do not have enough people of color[57] in your life and are definitely part of the problem. So, four to five black friends becomes a signifier that you are the good kind of non-black person. You have black people in your life, but not so many that it feels like a fetish. Your black friends average around 4.5 because friendship is fluid and you need people to know that you're not counting those black

---

57   "Person" of "color," I should note, as of publication, is an inoffensive term, unlike "colored person," which is a very bad term we do not say anymore even though at one point it was an option on the US census!

people, just throwing out a ballpark. These black friends make up enough people to start a basketball team, share a large pizza, and fit into a midsize Subaru sedan, so of course you are one of the good ones.

To be clear, I am definitely projecting. I do not know what people are thinking; I get paid to ask questions, not give answers! If you are wondering what gives me the unique qualifications to write about the complex subject of race in America, the answer is: vibes. This is simply one black friend's opinion on the world according to her. That is it.

There are no rules to determine which black friend is the Race Relations Spokesperson™ at any given time. Sometimes all you need is a hit radio show where you disseminate misogynistic rhetoric that oppresses half the people that you claim to represent. Other times the title goes to a black celebrity making a splash with a signature style of some sort—perhaps they have an iconic Afro, a signature mustache, or a notable vest. Sometimes these black celebrities are overqualified to discuss race in a thoughtful manner, and other times these black celebrities have one movie credit from the '90s that they are still riding within an inch of its life. Yet, at any given moment, if you turn on cable news you will find a black friend with a microphone speaking on behalf of all black people. This is harmful, reductive, and also incredibly profitable for any black friend who mainstream media decides is the Spokesperson that week. But just as a singular black friend can't absolve someone from looking racist, a black friend can't represent a complex community.

How many black friends do you have? The follow-up question is "Who wants to know and why?" Context ebbs and flows, yet we participate in this collective performance that stokes as much ire as it does admiration.

if beale street could talk, it would cuss you out

Ziwe: *Okay, Caroline Calloway, can you name five black people?*

Caroline Calloway: *Absolutely. Toni Morrison. Zora Neale Hurston. Maya Angelou. Oprah Winfrey. Fredless . . . Frederick Douglass. Those are my favorite authors. James Baldwin.*

Ziwe: *You read James Baldwin?*

Caroline Calloway: *Yes. Are you kidding?!*

Ziwe: *In public?*

Caroline Calloway: *I feel like I am the only white person ever who read* If Beale Street Could Talk *before it became a movie.*

Ziwe: *You're giving yourself too much credit, but, sure.*[58]

---

58   Excerpt from interview with Caroline Calloway, June 18, 2020, on Instagram Live.

I love free stuff.[59] I go to Christmas parties not for the social connections and holiday cheer but for the unlimited supply of jumbo shrimp and cocktail sauce. I do not particularly like Christmas,[60] but I love that once a year, companies, most of which refuse to offer their employees health care, throw lavish holiday parties with top-shelf liquor, celebrity DJs, and gift bags full of stale candy canes.[61] Before the pandemic, I would hit up two to three holiday parties a week for the full month of December, just to avoid having to pay for my own dinner. In my ideal world, these parties would be redistributed evenly throughout the year, but jamboree socialism™ is a political ideology reserved for the alternate timeline where Bernie Sanders is president.

At these events you pay for the freebies with your time (or in some cases your emotional labor). Whether that is listening to a boring panel in exchange for an open bar or tolerating unpleasant

---

59 When you're famous you get a lot of things for free. It seems like circular logic, because when most people become celebrities they can afford the designer things that they are now gifted. On a podcast, publicist and *America's Next Top Model* judge Kelly Cutrone discussed how some celebrities get to live in their apartments for free or at a deeply discounted rate because it brings clout to a building to hear that "Jessica Biel" or "Petey Pablo" or "Billy Graham Jr." lives in the building. Personally, I do not care if someone famous lives in my building; I just care whether or not my packages get stolen. Still, I have not reached this level of success yet, though I want a free apartment more than anything I've ever wanted in my life. But I digress. Mostly, this footnote is meant to express that my love language is gifts.

60 I actually grew up loving Christmas as a child, but then one day, maybe two years after I found out Santa wasn't real, I realized that not only were my parents paying for gifts, but they were financially sacrificing to make sure that I had the best commercial holiday their money could buy. This was a lot of pressure to put on a Furby that I only enjoyed for three weeks before I realized it did not do anything but make noises and be nosy. As a preteen, I watched a lot of local news, which consisted almost entirely of tragic stories about people losing their homes in a combination forest fire/flood, thus ruining Christmas for their children forever. As a result, I associate Christmas with disappointment. I wish that the day were not so closely tied with consumption and the vacuous void it is unable to fill. Anyway, be sure to add *Black Friend* by Ziwe to your wish list. The book is perfect for Hanukkah, Kwanzaa, Christmas, Winter Solstice, Eid, or whatever you and your loved ones celebrate during the holiday season.

61 Obviously, dental insurance would be better, especially if you're eating processed sugar.

small talk to justify filling your Tupperware with buffet leftovers, the unwritten rule is that you shouldn't complain about your experience because the service is complimentary.[62]

There are few things as gratifying as free food, but one offering that comes close is a screening of a movie that has not yet been released to the general public.

It saves money on ticket prices, which can cost as much as fifty dollars, depending on the film, its viewing time, and the ease with which you can sneak snacks in.[63] Also, there is no greater flex than inserting yourself into a conversation to express your opinions on a critically acclaimed movie that no one else has seen.

You'd say something like, "I love Jonny Greenwood's score in *Phantom Thread*, PTA[64] is such a force."

And then everyone around you would say something like, "Oh, I have not seen it yet, but I cannot wait."

---

62   You get what you pay for, unless you're counting taxes, and then you just have to accept that most public infrastructure is on the verge of collapse. Shoutout to the Brooklyn-Queens Expressway (allegedly)!

63   The easiest theater I've snuck food into is Magic Johnson Theater in Harlem, which is also the best movie theater I've ever been to. The acoustics and seating are great, but the biggest draw is the environment. I saw *Straight Outta Compton* there during opening weekend. Half of the audience arrived an *hour* into the movie. The other half of people, myself included, brought plates of jerk oxtail and malt liquor from the neighboring buffet spot. Everyone talked during the whole film. It was the most communal watching experience I have ever paid to participate in—I highly recommend.

64   That is Paul Thomas Anderson, for those of you not well versed in Cinema™ Discourse™. Fun fact: He is in a relationship with *Saturday Night Live* alumna Maya Rudolph, which makes them the most artistic couple in the world.

Which is when you would end the conversation by
saying, "Oh, it's not out yet, I went to a private screening,"
pretension sucking all of the air out of the room.

Everyone would be jealous of you, which would
technically make you the most powerful person in
that room until someone else casually hints at their
generational wealth.[65]

Being the first person in a friend group to see a movie offers major
clout, and taking advantage of free stuff is just good economics,
which is why I did not hesitate to attend an early screening of Barry
Jenkins's adaptation of James Baldwin's *If Beale Street Could Talk*
hosted by [REDACTED].[66]

I used to go to these screenings all the time. It is pretty simple:
You get an email. You register online. You go to the event. You tell
them your name. You sit down. You watch the movie. This is not
rocket science, folks; a monkey could do it if he had a working
Wi-Fi connection. But for some reason, getting into this screening
of *If Beale Street Could Talk* was harder than infiltrating the VIP
section of Up & Down on Rihanna night.[67]

---

65 They would say something like, "Sailing lessons! Summering on the Cape! The two best
days in a boat owner's life are the day they buy a boat and the day they sell it."

66 This name is redacted because the point of this story is not to call out a particular organization but rather to make an example of a fundamental misreading of James Baldwin's work.

67 Once upon a time, I was a little teenybopper who would put on my sheer American
Apparel dress and hop from the Boom Boom Room to Le Bain to the Jane to Up & Down in
one night. I would not say that I had fun partying, but it was something to do. The last time
I was at Up & Down, I was in the VIP section with a bunch of rappers and models whose
names you would recognize unless you spent your days watching *The 700 Club* on the Trinity
Broadcasting Network. Here are the most notable aspects of what I remember about that VIP
section: (1) It was just a platform maybe two inches from the ground separated from the general public by a thin rope, (2) it was too loud to hear anyone speak, (3) the best part was facing

My friend and I got to the venue forty-five minutes early because we wanted to secure good seats, as there is no point in watching a movie if you have to crane your neck from the front row.[68] Nothing would feel worse than reactivating childhood scoliosis while crying at the poetic words of James THEE Baldwin. My friend and I were the first attendees there. Anyone who is habitually early[69] knows sometimes you show up so early you have to watch the people working the event set up. This is awkward for the kind of person who feels the need to offer a helping hand, but I do not volunteer free labor, so for me it is not an issue. After about fifteen minutes, the screening attendant located the table (???) she needed to begin checking off the guest list as the formerly empty lobby filled up.

Finally, she was ready. Before checking us in, the attendant made the presumptuous announcement that members of the NAACP would be seated only after all members of [REDACTED] had claimed their tickets for *If Beale Street Could Talk.*

---

out seeing all the other people not in VIP wishing they were in VIP knowing that VIP is mid, and (4) other people's bottle service. One time at a famous weekly comedy show's afterparty, my friend bought a bottle of Belvedere that cost $1,300 from bottle service. It surprised me to see someone waste that money on literal poison (no offense). Still, I drank the drinks because, as you remember, I love free stuff. Another time when I was at Up & Down, a famous rapper kept dropping $100 bills on the floor. Like a fool, I tried to give him his money back, but he pretended I did not exist because I was my hotter friend's plus-one. As an underemployed recent graduate, I pocketed the money and spent it on one (1) monthly Metrocard. These stories sort of encompass my clubbing experiences: aimless but memorable.

68   I am not sure why the front seats of movies exist, and it is my personal belief that they should be sold at a heavily discounted rate (read: free!).

69   I like to be early for things because I get anxiety when people have to wait for me. It is disrespectful of other people's time. However, recently I have learned that making other people wait for you is a sign of power. It exemplifies superstardom. As Julie Andrews once said in the Criterion Collection classic *The Princess Diaries,* "A queen is never late; everyone else is simply early." Some of your fave stars will show up three hours late to a scheduled event and impress everyone with their cavalier approach to time zones. I have made some attempts to wield my power by showing up to events ten minutes early instead of thirty minutes early. My power has only increased incrementally . . .

She stared at us.

We stared at her.

We were the only black people there.

I should have openly protested that moving black attendees to the back of the figurative bus for the comfort and convenience of a predominantly *non-black* organization was contradictory to James Baldwin's life's work. But instead I thought, *James Baldwin is rolling in his grave.*

I was not a member of the National Association for the Advancement of Colored People, so while I knew this behavior was wrong, I did not invest in the problematic racial politics too much because they did not directly affect me.

Finally ready to admit the audience, the attendant asked for my membership card, which I did not ever carry with me because women's wallets are smaller.[70] Instead I told the attendant my name, which she loudly stated was *not on the list*. I was extremely triggered by this exchange to my teenybopper days when I used to fight other long-legged women to get into sections at Hotel Chantelle. But this time, the gatekeeper stood between me and a beautiful adaptation of a love story set in Harlem by one of the greatest American authors of all time, who, I should *remind*, was black.

---

70 Women's clothing is not functional. I can fit only about three bills and a driver's license in my wallet before it busts at the seams. Anyway, who carries their membership cards with them unless they are seeking AARP discounts? Fun fact: I recently learned on TikTok that an AARP membership is available to people of all ages for as low as $12 per year. Do with that what you will.

IN THIS ECONOMY?

Modern technology precludes any
need for me to search the forests
for beans or berries or whatever
forests have to offer aside from nosy
bearded men in their Teva sandals.
Instead, I comb the wilderness of
the internet searching for websites
like CouponCabin.com, which
is owned by Scott Kluth of Real
Housewife of New York Tinsley
Mortimer's ex fame, and then I
click each respective code, which
is hidden for some reason probably
involving data mining, and I reveal
and then copy and paste the code
in the respective website's discount
code box, and then I wait to see if
the fruits that I have reaped will
sustain me or if I must go back
and scavenge further in a never-
ending search for fulfillment. This
is my plight. Copy-and-pasting
code words like "THANKYOU"
and "FREESHIPPING" and
"BLACKFRIDAY" in the middle of
the spring (to no avail) on the off
chance that I break through and get
some savings. Knowing full well that
if I wanted to really avoid paying the
full price of an item I could simply
not buy it. But resisting nature is
easier than it sounds. Some people
are born to catch salmon with their
bare hands. Not I. I am born to
forage for markdowns at the risk
of being an uninformed consumer.
This is my story. This is my song.
This is my plight. I am the Coupon
Queen.

This was *oppression.*

This was *tyranny.*

This was a prescient metaphor for my obstacles as a young black
writer struggling to gain access to predominantly white spaces.[71]

---

71 At this moment in my life, I had been Twitter famous for years. As most online black
creators can attest to, there is not much upside in being famous on the internet. There was a
time when you could find my jokes rounded up on BuzzFeed, in *New York* magazine, the *Washington Post*, and so on, but I was struggling to get a writing job because I did not have enough
experience. It took a black woman to finally hire me for my first TV writing job after years of
trying. Thus, any sort of gatekeeper, especially one who is keeping me away from a movie written by a black author adapted by a black filmmaker, enraged me.

And it was particularly annoying because the people behind us who were late (read: technically on time but later than me) began to mumble in the way New Yorkers do when they have to wait for anything.[72] So, not only was I embarrassed, but I was also being subjugated, at least according to my ego.

I had gone to enough of these screenings to know that such entry hiccups were part of the cost of getting into free stuff. It was always a game of cat and mouse, Sam and Diane, Will They or Will They Not (Let Me into This Damn Event Space!), where the attendant said my name was not on the list because they did not hear or spell it correctly, only to locate my name and usher me into a glorious world of motion pictures. I get a sick satisfaction out of watching someone think they are right only to be proven wrong by cold hard facts. I never get an apology, but the sweet gratification of watching them fix that stupid look on their fugly face helps me sleep at night.

I knew I had registered for the movie online so there would inevitably be a paper trail. Of course, when I checked my email, I could not find my ticket.[73]

I tried to peek behind her makeshift table to scan the list, which was when the attendant repeated, "Any members of the NAACP

---

72 The city collectively suffers from attention deficit disorder. A large part of being a New Yorker is being mad at people who inconvenience you and being mad at the people who are mad at you for inconveniencing them. We are powered by a *"Fuck me? No, fuck you!"* energy, and if New Yorkers were to ever chill, the city would swallow itself whole.

73 Have you ever noticed that when you need to find something in your email, that is the exact moment when all records of it disappear? It is sort of like when you need to use your printer and suddenly it is out of paper and ink, and also broken. In conclusion, technology is bad.

must step aside and wait for all members of [REDACTED] to claim their ticket."

She glared at me again.

I stepped aside.

I was pretty sure this attendant thought I was a member of the NAACP because I was black. I can say this with confidence because every time she said "NAACP," she looked me dead in my colored-people eyes.

I tried to explain that I was not a member, even showing her that I was on the homepage of [REDACTED]'s website as a bastion of their pride in diversity . . . But she was more focused on letting each gray-haired, *New Yorker* tote-bag-toting latecomer get better seats than me as I stood in the wings with the separate but equal line of other black people who had to wait to see the James Baldwin movie.

Remember, racism is inconvenient.[74] On its worst days, this inconvenience can be fatal, but on its best days, and racism doesn't exactly have any good days, it results in taking the long way home or paying an egregious fine or traveling on the back of the bus even though you're tired and the bus is empty. I would not say that I was the Rosa Parks of this free screening of *If Beale Street Could Talk*, but one could make that comparison and I would not protest.[75]

---

74   Especially to me personally!

75   Only Rosa Parks is the Rosa Parks of Montgomery busing discrimination. I like to compare myself to civil rights figures because I find it to be so laughably offensive. One time, PETA compared their fight for animal rights to Martin Luther King Jr.'s fight for civil rights. Adopt

I was plotting how I could ruin this screening for everyone (*perhaps I'd pull a fire alarm or call in a bomb threat?*) when I decided to check my email one last time. And of course, there it was. The ticket had been registered under "Ziwe F" because I was too lazy to write my full last name on Eventbrite's mobile app. (A mistake that I will admit is my fault, but the political optics of this are still perilous!) By this point, almost every blond and brunette attendee had been seated. I raced back in line and showed the attendant my ticket as a member of [REDACTED]. This surprised her; I cannot say why (though I know what my first guess would be). But somehow, she still could not find my name on the list, so I took her stupid piece of paper and scanned it until I found the name "Ziwe," which took about five seconds because it was the only name that started with a Z. She said—and folks, this made me blind with rage—"Oops, I must have missed it."

---

don't shop, fur is murder, blah blah blah, all that stuff . . . I love animals, do not get me wrong, but there is no way that Hello Kitty has done anything as iconic as writing "Letters from a Birmingham Jail." Far too often, you'll find a well-meaning black leader compared to Martin Luther King Jr. or Barack Obama or Rosa Parks, but the truth is . . . there is only one Martin Luther King Jr. There is only one Barack Obama. There is only one Rosa Parks. A fact I realize isn't as widely circulated is that Rosa Parks was not the first black person to refuse to sit in the back of the bus. Many black people made these same protests, and they were similarly arrested. In fact, nine months before Rosa Parks refused, there was a black teen named Claudette Colvin who was on her way home from school when she was asked to vacate her seat for a couple of white women. A member of the NAACP Youth Council, Claudette was young and dark skinned, and had been impregnated by an older man by the age of sixteen. Although Claudette was clearly a victim of segregation, black leadership had decided that she was not the perfect victim to rally a national movement against racism behind. Eventually, that perfect figure came in the form of Rosa Parks, NAACP secretary and forty-two-year-old seamstress, about nine months after Claudette's arrest, which prompted the Montgomery Bus Boycott that we know today. Still, Claudette made history, as her federal lawsuit, *Browder vs. Gayle*, challenged the constitutionality of Montgomery segregation, paving the way for the success of Montgomery bus integration. This is all to say that there are so many overlooked instances of defiance that are equally important in the fight for liberation . . . and my encounter at this screening is one of them.

Oops.

I

Must

Have

Missed

It.

How dare she? During Black History Month,[76] no less!

My friend and I had to wait an hour to get seated at the Barry Jenkins adaptation of James Baldwin's *If Beale Street Could Talk* with the other black people who were not members of [REDACTED]. The truth is, it was just as unfair for the members of the NAACP to wait for admission as it was for me. Just because I was a paying member of [REDACTED], did not mean I was entitled to better seats. In the grand scheme of oppression, this does not register on the suffering scale. But why was there tiered seating in the first place? Who was this free screening intended to benefit? Sure, it's only fair that paying members of [REDACTED] get to reap the benefits of their membership, but why invite the NAACP to serve as black friends in the first place if you were going to put them last, especially at an event that centered around their blackness? Was this a meaningful partnership or an empty performative gesture? When events are free, the expectation is that you get what you

---

76 It was not Black History Month. But it was Black History Month Energy.

pay for. That beggars can't be choosers. But, why can't beggars be choosers? Why couldn't we sit and enjoy the movie from the back aisle seat, as I intended? For me, it was because the attendant was so entrenched in her perceived idea of me that she could not be bothered to listen. But for every other black person at that screening, it was because they were not as valuable to the screening as the paying members of [REDACTED].

So, that day we all found ourselves craning our necks from the front row. I bet if Beale Street could talk, it would cuss them out.

The conflict with corporate allyship is that freedom is marketable, but everything else involving race is not. Every January, my inbox fills with requests from companies looking to "celebrate" my "identity" during Black History Month. One job asked me to spotlight a black woman from history, so I chose my hero, Ida B. Wells. I spoke about how as cofounder of the NAACP, Ida B. Wells had won a posthumous Pulitzer Prize for her revolutionary journalism documenting lynchings in the American South, creating one of the country's first known databases. Soon after I submitted this spotlight, the company flagged that I kept mentioning "lynching" when I described Wells's work. They thought it was too jarring for their Black History Month festivities. I did not know how to explain to these kind, wonderful benefactors that the unpleasant "lynching" part was unfortunately the "history" part. The company and I went back and forth on this, and suddenly I understood the subtext. They wanted blackness without having to deal with black people. They wanted the blues without the strange fruit hanging from the poplar tree. Black History Month, but make it commercial. This was not the first time in my career that I had heard these instructions. In fact, it was an obstacle I faced every day. A decade of these battles had taught me when to choose them. I kept my message short and palatable.

Years later, when interviewing Drew Barrymore for a Miss Universe–themed episode, I tried to give Ida B. Wells her proper due.

> **Drew Barrymore:** *Who is your hero going back?*
>
> **Ziwe:** *Ida B. Wells. If we're talking about American journalism, she is one of the pathfinders.*
>
> **Drew Barrymore:** *That's my daughter's other favorite person!*
>
> **Ziwe:** *Shut up, you know who Ida B. Wells is?*
>
> **Drew Barrymore:** *Yes!*
>
> **Ziwe and Drew Barrymore:** *[chanting] Ida B. Wells! Ida B. Wells! Ida B. Wells!*
>
> **Ziwe:** *And that's our show. Drew Barrymore, everyone! What a star!*
>
> **Ziwe and Drew Barrymore:** *[chanting] Ida B. Wells! Ida B. Wells! Ida B. Wells! Ida B. Wells!*
>
> *(graphics appear on lower third of screen)*
>
> *IDA FACT: PIONEERING FIGURE IN AMERICAN JOURNALISM!*
>
> *IDA FACT: CREATED A DATABASE OF LYNCHINGS IN 1892*
>
> *IDA FACT: CO-FOUNDED THE NAACP!*[77]

I bet if Beale Street could talk, it would cuss me out.

---

77   Excerpt from interview in *ZIWE* S2 E11, "Miss Universe with Drew Barrymore," December 18, 2022, on Showtime.

cancel culture

Ziwe: Okay, so we have two more questions for you. One question for, one question for you is, people have been canceling you say since the eighties; what do you think about cancel culture? It is, so when, like, is it okay to cancel someone if they've committed a hate crime? Where does it end, where does it begin?

Alyssa Milano: If they've committed a hate crime, of course.

Ziwe: Sure. Okay. Yeah, that's a good place to take a stand.

Alyssa Milano: So . . . but the thing about cancel culture that I think is so interesting is like we're not really canceling these people, right? Like, like if, if they had succeeded when they had tried to cancel me and, you know, decades ago, I wouldn't still be here I think. I think it's kind of become like its own, it sort of has its own identity, what cancel culture is, right? Like it kind of breathes its own life of, it's something specific, like you fucked up, and I'm going to call you out on it, which isn't really canceling someone, right? It's, it's giving people the opportunity to be able to see where you may have fucked up.[78]

---

78   Excerpt from interview with Alyssa Milano, July 16, 2020, on Instagram Live.

Megyn Kelly tried to cancel me. On June 15, 2021, she tweeted a three-page (!!!) letter written by Gabriela Baron, a parent who pulled her eighth-grader out of the Spence School[79] because a teacher showed a clip of my show in class.

The caption read, "(Another) Spence parent pulls her kid after grossly racist episode attacking white women is forced on girls in class on last day of school. We just left this school bc of its growing far-left indoctrination. This is a place we've loved—breaks my heart they're doing this."

In her letter, Baron wrote:

> This evening, we learned that yesterday, during our daughter's last history class, the class was shown a video by Ziwe which exemplifies hate speech against white women. My husband and I watched the video in its entirety and were shocked. The video openly derides, humiliates and ridicules white women. It is punctuated at regular intervals by fake ads, which are part of the video's editorial content and were shown to the class, that end with the slogan "White Women." There are two fake ads in the video of white women touching each other and kissing that were not shown to the class, but the remainder of the video was shown.[80]

---

79   For context, the all-girls private school located on the Upper East Side of Manhattan has a tuition of about $50,000. It has a homogenous student demographic.

80   The two women kissing were critically acclaimed actresses Jane Krakowski and Cristin Milioti, in a parody commercial for American Girl dolls.

Rather than describe the video, I ask that you all watch it for yourselves. Unlike the students in my daughter's class, you have a choice as to what you watch. The fact that our daughters do not have that choice is all the more reason why you should take the time to see what was deemed worthy of our children's time and attention in a Spence classroom. It is available on Showtime (you can search for Ziwe and it is Episode 1: "55%") or online at https://www.sho.com/ziwe/season/1.

This cancellation was the best advertisement for my show that money couldn't buy. I do not like stoking the conservative outrage machine, because I have an aversion to death threats. However, at this point, Megyn Kelly was far past her height. The former Fox News host was now just a famous podcaster. I was not afraid of her. If anything, I was more insulted by the private school issuing an apology that said "Sharing a satirical video that made fun of white women was a significant mistake." First of all, my show didn't make fun of white women; it celebrated people of all races, especially those with melanin differences. While there was no part of my show that advertised itself as appropriate for an eighth-grade social studies class, my *jokes* were no more offensive than anything that's ever happened in American history. I would like to cancel the Spence School for not defending me, a fellow coastal elite private school graduate. Then, I would like to cancel myself for going to private school. And then, I would like to cancel Megyn Kelly for her entire career, but specifically for the moment when she insisted that Santa Claus, who is a fictional mythical being, is white when he is obviously mixed. I wish I could cancel us all, but I don't believe in cancel culture.

Cancel culture has been co-opted to encompass too many things at once for it to have any real meaning. Getting canceled because you tweeted "I hate BTS"[81] is different from getting canceled because you made your employees watch you masturbate. These things could not be further apart, yet they've been lumped under one cultural phenomenon. The fact that "cancel culture" reflects a wide range of social interactions delegitimizes criticism that holds people in power accountable. Now when someone rich and powerful is "canceled" for the "politically incorrect" behavior of "committing a hate crime," he claims he's experiencing a biased witch hunt meant to undercut all the old men who have bright futures.

I don't believe in cancel culture; however, I do believe that people should be held accountable for their actions. The problem is that public outrage has a short memory. I have seen some of the most cancelable men of my generation rebound in indie movies that go on to be nominated for prestigious awards. And the same people whose lives were "ruined" return as titans of industry after laying low in their mansions for a couple of years. So rarely do the ramifications of cancel culture extend past an internet connection. And when they do, it is important to remember that they usually result in an incredibly privileged person temporarily experiencing slightly less privilege than they were accustomed to, which is still a very high baseline of privilege compared with the rest of the world. Personally, I long to be a canceled rich man because that is just a vacation.

It is hard to talk about cancel culture without discussing one of my most iconic guests, Alison Roman, a food writer, chef, and success-

---

81 I should note that I do not believe this and anyone who does is stupid and wrong. Please don't cancel me.

ful author who gained popularity for her accessible personality and simplistic cooking videos. Over the course of her career, she held front-facing positions at *Bon Appétit*, BuzzFeed Food, and *New York Times Cooking*. But just as her career was hitting its stride, she was canceled by "This You?"[82] Twitter after she was quoted in a niche internet newsletter calling Chrissy Teigen and Marie Kondo "sellouts."

Roman's critics were quick to note that her ire was directed mostly at Asian women, despite some of her most popular recipes featuring Asian cuisine. To many, she represented the privilege that allowed white people to capitalize on cultures they did not belong to. In her case it was with bestselling cookbooks with recipes like Shortcut Chilaquiles, Chicken Tikka Masala, and Tangy Braised Short Ribs, which she emphasized in the recipe were different from Korean short ribs.

Soon, she became the face of cultural appropriation in food media. While she did not have institutional power, individually, she was

---

82   "This You?" is a social media community on Twitter that has better investigative skills than Sherlock Holmes on 60 milligrams of Adderall. While they have been known to get it wrong at times (because the internet doesn't usually fact-check until after things have gone viral), the "This You?" community excels at calling out individuals and companies for their hypocrisy using undeniable screenshots. To be in the "This You?" community's line of fire is to have a miserable day/week/month online. You never want to be their main character.

We can all agree that "angry" "mobs" are objectively bad. Doxxing is "objectively" "bad." Yet . . . there is something cathartic about vigilante justice. The problem is with the evolution of groups like Stan Twitter; these vigilantes overreach acting less like Batman and more like the Joker's gang of indiscriminate clowns antagonizing anyone who crosses their path. I wish I had an army of keyboard killers to check anyone who dares slander my name like Nicki's Barbz, Taylor's Swifties, or Beyoncé's BeyHive (infantries that for my safety I must note that I am an active member of). I am not sure what I could call my stans—Ziwe's icons, perhaps? But what I do know is that great power comes with great responsibility. Unfortunately, most Stans appear to be in high school and love sending death threats. These child soldiers reflect the best and worst of "This You?" The best part is that they can represent diverse communities coming together under one shared interest. The worst part is that they unfortunately quell free speech to promote unwavering fealty to their (cult) leaders.

a beneficiary of it. And with her story as the gateway, dominoes began to fall, calling out very prominent companies as well.

The George Floyd protests led to a cultural shift in accountability. Gone were the days of companies remaining quiet to protect their bottom line. Corporations (and their offshore subsidiaries) took to social media to declare that "racism is very bad." Some of these declarations were in good faith, but others seemed to conveniently preempt scandal.

PAPA JOHNS
> Our hearts go out to our black employees, communities, and friends. We stand with you against racism and injustice. We will continue to work to drive change.

It takes a certain level of bravery to stand up against injustice when less than a year before mass protests began, the founder of Papa Johns, Mr. Papa John himself, allegedly used the n-word in a conference call about [*checks notes*] preventing future public-relations crises. Of course, it is not fair to judge a brand for its namesake and former CEO's actions in the very recent past. God is working on us all; no one is perfect!

GUSHERS

> Gushers would not be Gushers without the Black community and your voices. We're working with @fruitbythefoot on creating space to amplify that. We see you. We stand with you

I, for one, am proud to live in a country that celebrates diversity like it celebrates the fruit-flavored assortment in a Gushers variety pack. I can sleep easy at night knowing that Gushers recognizes the black community's contribution to the production, distribution, and ingestion of high fructose corn syrup in food deserts. This is where reparations begin—forty Gushers and a Capri Sun.

SAN FRANCISCO 49ERS

Black Lives Matter #BlackoutTuesday 🖤

Now, did the San Francisco 49ers fire Colin Kaepernick for peacefully protesting police brutality, rendering this demonstration of solidarity at best, hollow, and at worst, offensive? The answer is debatable if you are a libel lawyer interested in suing me. When it comes to anti-racism, it's the thought that counts . . . and the thought behind this post is . . . decontextualized, because there is no text attached to this post other than #BlackoutTuesday.[83]

---

83   On June 2, 2020, thousands of people posted a black square with the hashtag #blackouttuesday, as an initiative to go silent on social media and stand in solidarity with the Black Lives Matter movement. This campaign was started by Jamila Thomas and Brianna Agyemang, music industry executives, who wrote in an open letter that their "mission is to hold the industry at large, including major corporations + their partners who benefit from the efforts, struggles and success of black people accountable." However, at the time this genesis and intention were less clear, as Instagram users uninvolved in the entertainment industry included #blacklivesmatter as they posted their little black squares. In doing so, they did the opposite of going silent online by flooding the #blacklivesmatter tag. Instead, they suppressed thousands of images that activists used to mobilize protests. This symbolic gesture was done to demonstrate solidarity, but in actuality it was just a photo of a Pantone color (#19-0303 TCX, to be exact). By 12:00 P.M., there was a strong legion of people, most notably Representative Alexandria Ocasio-Cortez, explaining exactly what was wrong with these #BlackoutTuesday photos. This prompted many people I knew to delete the black photo entirely or delete and repost the photo without the hashtag. But the damage had been done. This unintended consequence of performing unity exemplifies the ways in which people can mean well and still do absolutely wrong. Best-case scenario, the black square shows your network that you at least care about black people enough to post a photo, which I should note is free and easy. Unfortunately, worst-case scenario, this insignificant action can set forth a tidal wave of trouble for the grassroots activists on the ground doing the work. Performing solidarity is inherently

THE DEFINITIVE ANTI-RACISM GUIDE, ACCORDING TO A CORPORATE PROFITEER

Step 1: Accept that everything you've ever read has been neo-capitalist propaganda. Except for this book.

Step 2: Hop onto the nearest soapbox and declare "I AM A PROUD RACIST" to anyone who will listen. People will stop and stare because they are jealous of your emotional breakthrough.

Step 3: Do the real work of unlearning the very foundation upon which society was built. This should take a couple of days, or however long it takes for you to skim bell hooks's entire complete works.

Step 4: Document your journey on Instagram, Twitter (RIP), TikTok, and/or LinkedIn for your respective personal and professional networks to appreciate your moderate radicalization.

Step 5: Change your profile picture to an unlicensed illustration of a victim of a hate crime. Do not remove this photo until racism is over or you've taken a selfie that better reflects your aesthetic.

Step 6: Educate your extended family on their shortcomings as racists, unless those family members grew up during a "different time," like the early 2000s.

Step 7: Cut out all the bigots in your inner circle until you have no friends. Remember that the answer to why you were surrounded by so many racists in the first place is a question for a different year.

Step 8: Confess to any black person who will listen that your paternal grandmother still says the n-word. They do not want this information, but this catharsis is for you, not them.

Step 9: Attend one (1) protest and fall deeply, madly in love with another protester holding a sign that says "IF [INSERT DEMOCRAT] WAS PRESIDENT WE'D BE AT BRUNCH RIGHT NOW."

Step 10: Have children with this young revolutionary, gentrify an up-and-coming neighborhood, and complain about the lack of diversity to other members of your co-op board.

Step 11: Let the healing begin.

Where businesses could hide behind press releases and the launch of multiracial Band-Aids, individuals had nowhere to go. And for good reason. It is much easier to ask, "Why did you have a wedding on a plantation?" than it is to ask, "How can we break up that plantation and give the land to the ancestors of the formerly enslaved people who built it?"[84] It is much easier to ask, "Why did you, a non-Asian person, agree to play the role of an Asian person?" than it is to ask, "Why would the studio insist on casting a non-Asian person as their lead actor in a global release?" Blaming individuals is fun; deconstructing centuries of oppression requires so much boring reading. One tactic is like getting stitches, and the other is like getting a transplant of every vital organ—even if the face is the same, it is a totally different person.

This is how I approached interviewing Alison Roman. She was an individual in a system that admonished her for behavior that even three months prior she was rewarded for. Did she change or did the system? Or did nothing really change at all?

I read her apology and thought, If I had to apologize for racism, I would plagiarize this. So, I asked her about it.

---

selfish. Its very point is to virtue-signal that you are a good person, because it matters to you that people know you are a good person. The problem is that people who are suffering do not get paid in thoughts and prayers. If you really want to effect actual change, you have to look into your arsenal of talents that you can sustain longer than a social media day. Can you sing? Can you write? Can you build a cabinet? Are you good at organizing networks of people? Are you charismatic and convincing enough to effectively phonebank for underfunded candidates? Are you a social recluse with deep pockets that can fund charitable organizations? Are you bad at everything? There is a job for everyone. I am a well-spoken, attractive person, so my job is to be hot and loudly repeat things that smarter people say. If there is one thing we have learned from 2020, it is that incremental change takes time and the fight for liberation is a lifelong commitment, not a trend.

84   See—too many words!

Ziwe: Oh my God. Thank you. Now. Let's just start it off because I actually think that you wrote one of the best apologies in white-people apology tours.

Alison Roman: Mmm-hmm.

Ziwe: That is, in the last three to six months. So, my question for you is, "How many women of color helped you write that apology?"

Alison Roman: Um, I had three friends that I sent various drafts to that like really helped me sort of get to not only like general understanding of the things that I was actually apologizing for but like, they are also—it was not like they were necessarily like telling me what to say, but they are like, "Here's why you need to say this" and like getting me to a very baseline of understanding of what I was actually apologizing for because I was not interested in like a vague general like "learning growing" bullshit, like I really wanted to like grasp why it was that I was even writing in the first place.

Ziwe: Totally. And did you pay these women of color for their emotional labor?

Alison Roman: I sent them all gifts in person—

Ziwe: Wow.

Alison Roman: And then in the mail as well and handwritten cards. Yeah.

Ziwe: Okay. I love, I love—

Alison Roman: I also, I made donations to several organizations in their name like as a thank-you like to different—especially like focusing on Asian-American organizations that were helping people with immigration issues with their families or stuff like that.

Ziwe: No, I love that. That is great to hear. Now, speaking of Asian Americans, why do you hate Asian women?[85]

85   Excerpt from interview with Alison Roman, June 25, 2020, on Instagram Live.

She approached my questions at face value, despite the fact that in any court of law, she could reject the premise of these questions as entrapment. Every individual is allowed to have their own take-away from this exchange, but my takeaway was that this discourse around race was foreign, even to me. I was nervous about the prospect of talking to her because I could not accept an apology on behalf of the community she harmed. I am famously not an Asian woman, and thus I have no authority to assess the credibility of her words addressed to Asian women.

Here, we saw that my guest was doing the work™ of listening, accepting accountability, and donating her resources. But why was she apologizing? Because she was genuinely sorry or because she was sorry she got caught? Is that enough penance from an individual who would've continued to benefit if not for a cultural shift? I do not know. Her apology could've just lived in the ether, but she added actions to her words, and allowed probing. Our conversation was not possible without both of us showing up, but the importance of the show depended on the thousands of users live-commenting during the stream.

Many commented on how anti-Asian sentiments were like the punch line of hate crimes, because people did not take them as seriously. This is because of the model minority myth, which posits that Asian Americans and Pacific Islanders are inherently high achieving and have overcome discrimination by pulling themselves up by their bootstraps. "They're not really marginalized." While falsely painting the Asian community as a monolith, it also serves to erase collective experiences of racial discrimination. While black and Asian Americans have been pitted against each other by the model minority myth, our communities have similarities.

In the spring of 2021, there was a hate crime in Georgia in which a white man went to three spas and killed eight people, six of them Asian women. In the aftermath of the killings, there was a press conference with Atlanta officials, who described what they knew of the suspect's intentions. The captain of the Cherokee County Sheriff's Office said,

> The suspect did take responsibility for the shootings. . . . He does claim that it was not racially motivated. He apparently has an issue, what he considers a sex addiction, and sees these locations as something that allows him to go to these places, and it is a temptation for him, that he wanted to eliminate. Like I said it is still early on. But those were comments that he made.

What are the politics of a police officer speaking on behalf of the murder suspect at an official presser standing behind the city seal? Who does this police officer represent? The people or the perpetrator?

The truth is, there are very few racists who would self-identify as racists. George Washington would not describe himself as a racist, but he'd wax poetic about freedom of speech with a mouth full of teeth he "allegedly" extracted from slaves. Racists do not get to decide whether or not their actions are racist. It is the rest of us who are subject to their outbursts who can stand back and connect the dots.

The callousness of describing the death of six Asian women as a "temptation" a mass murderer wanted to "eliminate" is racist. Perhaps the hate crime is not just the act of violence, but the context that predicates a young white man to walk into a spa and shoot up the place because he doesn't want to be horny anymore. I've been horny and I've never committed murder. But this man was socialized to associate arousal with Asian women and prioritize his feelings over their lives. Maybe it started with the same place that created the Japanese internment camps, passed the Chinese Exclusion Act, waged a war in Vietnam in the name of containment, and referred to COVID-19 as the "kung flu." This not-so-coded language dehumanizes victims in a way that serves only those who can relate to that hot blind rage. Misogyny and race, we see here, are intertwined.

The officer continued, "He was pretty much fed up. He was fed up, at the end of his rope . . . yesterday was a really bad day for him and this is what he did."

Again, who does this benefit? If anything, this language normalizes these violent actions to suggest that anyone could be a bad day away from a "racially motivated" killing spree.

This news aligned, absurdly, with season five of *The Real Housewives of Dallas*.[86] The central storyline of the season is that Brandi Redmond, a former Dallas Cowboys cheerleader, was canceled on social media for a racist video in which she pulled her eyes in a slant and imitated an Asian person. This criticism prompted Brandi Redmond to commit to a rehab center, as the trauma of this backlash made her want to die. She unloads all of this information on the show's first Asian housewife, Tiffany Moon, prompting a gracious Tiffany to say that she never got the impression that

---

86   *The Real Housewives of Dallas* somehow makes the case for segregation, because every single time the characters interact with the non-white characters they are really mean.

Brandi was racist after knowing her for less than six weeks. Tiffany clarifies that while Brandi's actions were hurtful, she knows they were not malicious.

It is hard to watch this emotional labor.

But not as hard to watch as what turns out to be a multiple-episode arc in which Brandi Redmond insists that she is not comfortable making jokes around Tiffany Moon because, as we learn through several testimonials, Tiffany is Asian. Tiffany expresses that if you are uncomfortable around her because she's Asian, that is not something she can change about herself, and ultimately it is Brandi's problem. This exchange is a metaphor for reality. Without any provocation at all, her existence is triggering.

I remember this distinct feeling during the summer of racial reckoning when people suddenly were deeply invested in black voices. On the one hand, it felt good to finally be signal boosted—this was the year the comedy I had been performing for years reached national discourse. But it all felt a little performative. It was hard to see people, in light of tragedy, start tagging Asian artists that "you should know about and follow." It should not take a hate crime for people to recognize the contributions that the Asian community has made to America.

Alison Roman, in her own way, was trying to make things better. Whether that was for herself or for the people she hurt, I do not know—but she offered answers to impossible questions. Is there room to admit to one's faults, even begrudgingly? I hope so.

Roman did not have institutional power, but individually, she was a beneficiary of it. While cancel culture prompted her unceremonious termination at several legacy media brands, from the outside looking in, Roman appears to be professionally thriving. She has a popular YouTube series and a recent *New York Times* bestselling cookbook.

In other words, she survived. And so did I. The outrage around my own controversial statements did not derail me. I believe the only cancel culture that's gone too far is Showtime's cancellation of my TV show. The companies that shared their public statements on race relations are still in business whether or not they effectively ended racism. (They did not!) The world still turns. If anything, commitments to parity that cancel culture catalyzed are in jeopardy as conservative organizations fight to ban the very acknowledgment of culture, as in the case of Florida's Don't Say Gay Woke Act.

I do not believe in cancel culture, but the occasional stupidity of its groupthink is a small price to pay for accountability.

just because you're racist doesn't mean you're a bad person

Being racist doesn't inherently make you a bad person; it just makes you racist.

I think people are too sensitive about the label. They've convinced themselves that the worst thing in the world you can call someone is a "racist," when in actuality the worst thing in the world you can call someone is a slur, including but not limited to the n-word, the f-word, the c-word, the r-word, the k-word, the g-word, or any other bad word I learned from watching six seasons of *The Sopranos*.

Don't get me wrong. I love Tony Soprano and all his gabagool. However, he introduced me to racial epithets I didn't know existed.

The truth is, there are a lot of technically lovely people in the world who are racist. They raise beautiful families and have good friends and are respected members of their community. They may do idyllic shit like play the clarinet or knit sweaters for a flock of malnourished ducks in their pool or some other hobby. Unfortunately, that doesn't take away the fact that their actions (or more often their inactions) are racist. This is easier than one might think, because for the past several centuries, racism has been in its slay era. Contrary to the mythos of 2020, it has given no indication that it'll die out. If anything, it's adapting.

Racists are not just cranky old people who are "products of their time." They are also young people with 5G data networks who have a penchant for holding sea bass in their dating profile picture. They are future judges. They are future taxidermists. They shape our ecosystem both large and small. They don't own a Klan hoodie or fly a Confederate flag. They are just regular people who happen to subscribe to one of the most dominant political tools of subjugation in world history. Because, again, it is far easier to be a racist than to not be one.

So, if someone calls you racist, don't be so hard on yourself! You are not a bad person; you are just someone whose entire existence propagates the oppression of billions of people. And, while who you are is not your fault, it is very much your responsibility.

reality

Ziwe: *What do you think of the fact that all three of the black Bachelors and Bachelorettes have ended up with, you know, partners not of color?*

Rachel Lindsay: *That is a great question; it is something I was worried about before I went on the show. I think I got a little more grace because I was the first, and people were just excited that a person of color was in this role, but then I think when the next person chose someone who was not black and then by the time we went to the third one it was like, you know what, they are just not going to choose anybody who was black. This is what I'll say to that. One, I do not think, I think it shows how unfairly people of color are held to certain standards that their white counterparts are not. On the other hand I will say, it is a casting issue. There was a point where I broke down on camera, and they used my tears for something else, but I was getting upset at the selection of men of color . . . And I also learned as I was going through my season that several of the black men on my season did not date black women.*

Ziwe: *Really??!*

Rachel Lindsay: *So there's that.*

Ziwe: *Let's unpack this.*

Rachel Lindsay: *The show found it interesting. Wow, this guy's never dated a black woman before. And I said, you think that is interesting? That is my life, I live that. That is why I am speaking out. You do not need to just diversify your cast and your leads, you need to diversify the people behind the camera.*[87]

I wanted to be the first black Bachelorette.

The role was not a stretch of my skill set by any means. I had always thought I'd be the first black president; however, Barack Obama beat me by about forty years. Naturally, the next-best step was having thirty greased-up meatheads clamoring for an over-the-pants handy in the fantasy suite. To my disappointment, I never achieved this goal. And what happens to a dream deferred? It goes to the black woman willing to do the grunt work of breaking institutional barriers. In this case, it was Rachel Lindsay, an accomplished attorney and daughter of Sam Lindsay, the first black judge to serve on the federal district court in Dallas. Rachel Lindsay for all intents and purposes reflected Du Bois's Talented Tenth. Acceptable and nonthreatening to what she described as a "lily white" audience.

Since her season, Lindsay has shared her mixed feelings about *The Bachelor*, ultimately thanking the hallowed American institution for the huge platform that catapulted her into millions of

---

87   Excerpt from interview in ZIWE S1 E2, "Beauty Standards with Rachel Lindsay," May 16, 2021, on Showtime.

homes. But in our conversation, she discussed how all of the black Bachelors and Bachelorettes who followed her ended up with non-black partners. Most notably was Matt James, formerly engaged to *Bachelor* contestant Rachael Kirkconnell. Fans criticized Kirkconnell for attending an "Old South Party,"[88] which then *Bachelor* host Chris Harrison defended, costing him his decades-long job as host of the hit show.

The Bachelor at its worst is a setting that reflects sexism and racism back onto its contestants through a ratings-obsessed production.[89] No self-respecting person would enter an unscripted arena knowing that their fate was completely left up to the amoral reality gods (e.g., producers and editors). Of course, when an "unrelated" dating show called me to guest-star on an episode, I took a twelve-hour flight from Paris to Los Angeles to tape a segment on a Sunday afternoon somewhere near Santa Clarita.

The first thing I noticed when I pulled up to the private ranch an hour away from my Beverly Hills hotel[90] was how dry the land was. I would say I have an irrational fear of wildfires, but it is rational to fear being swallowed whole by fire and burned alive. The last time I visited LA, I was at a cool Hollywood party where suddenly the host directed guests to look outside. Why? Because it was rain-

---

88   For the record, I do not understand why people attend these themed parties. What about a New South Party? The new South has internet and running water and Sonic milkshakes. The only thing notable about an "Old South Party" is slavery and Jim Crow. That is what was happening in the Old South. There is literally nothing different. It's still hot; they still have cobblestone streets; they still have mint juleps. But now there's air-conditioning. That's a privilege to throw a party about! No one is stopping you from walking around with a drawl, a petticoat, and a parasol on your shoulder. Seems like "Old South Party" just mourns that slavery is illegal? It will always be a red flag.

89   This was allegedly depicted in the Lifetime show *UnREAL*. Season 1 was great!

90   It was not the Beverly Hills Hotel, to be clear.

ing ash and if you tilted your head and hated Greta Thunberg, it looked like snow. Well, up in Santa Clarita, the grass was so brown it looked like it was dusted in cocoa powder. Everything appeared pale and lifeless, even the sprawling mountains. For twenty minutes, my SUV winded down a private, isolated road that very well could have driven me to my death. I wondered briefly if I was in the wrong place, until I saw a patch of plush pasture tended by what was probably an illegal sprinkler. I thought, *Isn't there a drought?*

I landed at my trailer and waited for what would be a wild eight-hour day. The producers debriefed me on all of the girls and drama and the "sexy" single man who was excited to meet me because he loved my interview with Adam Pally where I asked him if the cornrows he got for a movie were worth it.[91] The single man wanted me to practice the same confrontational line of questioning with him.

---

91   From *ZIWE*, episode 106, June 13, 2022:

Ziwe holds a photo of Adam in cornrows.

Ziwe (cont'd): This is a photo—

Adam: Okay.

Ziwe: That you're in. Explain how we got here, and is this allyship to the black community? Look at it. Look at it!

Adam: First of all, am I pulling it, pulling it off a little? With hair off my face you can see my face a little so it's like, it's not, no. Um. It was for a movie.

Ziwe: What movie?

Adam: Called *Dirty Grandpa*.

Ziwe: Was it worth it?

Adam: Absolutely not; nothing I've ever done was worth that. But Robert De Niro was in that movie, and I really wanted to work with him before he died.

Ziwe: Oh my god you can't say that, Adam! Before he died! He's still alive!

Adam: [whispers] What?

Ziwe: [whispers] Yeah. [Not whispering] So it sounds like it was worth it, appropriating my culture, thanks.

Adam: Okay—

Ziwe: No!

I get this request a lot.

I laughed.

Okay.

There were three main takeaways from shooting [REDACTED]:

1. *I was not always aware when cameras were rolling.*
    Because of this and the fact that we taped for several
    hours, I had a loose understanding of what I said. As
    someone who has produced a talk show, I understand
    that when people let their guard down they are honest.
    But as a performer, this is my single greatest fear, as
    there are several versions of an eight-hour shoot that
    could and would be cut down to a ten-minute segment.
    Which version of me would the producers show? The
    villainous interviewer with a sexist line of questioning or
    the sympathetic therapist who genuinely worried about
    the cast members' well-being?

2. *I was offered alcohol.* First a bottle of white wine, which
    was their mistake because I only drink red wine. The
    second time, I ordered a margarita with my lunch
    because I sensed they wanted me to have fun. I did not
    drink it, which a producer observed as we changed
    locations. I went back into my trailer and poured some of
    the margarita down the drain to make it look like I had
    some. The limes and mint clogged the sink, which I think
    is the no-win scenario. A younger me would have enjoyed

the free booze, but my work schedule sobered me. Plus, being drunk in the scorching sun where grass grew in spite of natural law seemed like a recipe for dehydration.

3. *The girls.* Or rather the young women who were referred to as "girls." They were ten years younger than me, and the position of power I held over them made me feel uncomfortable. As I interrogated them about whether they joined the competitive dating show that makes unknowns famous for the right reasons, I worried how they would come off if they were honest. I had an earpiece that allowed production to talk to me as I hosted my segment. Producers would feed me lines. Sometimes I would pretend I didn't hear them and other times I would repeat their words verbatim. Things moved so quickly that I could not edit my words for kindness. I moved at production's whim and the contestants/girlfriends/sisterwives moved at mine, which prompted some funny conversations about sex that I partially regret.

More so, it prompted introspection about my complicity in the arts of reality TV. Suzanne Collins created *The Hunger Games* as an examination of this genre. She once told Scholastic,

> *The Hunger Games* is a reality television program . . .
> An extreme one, but that's what it is. And while I think
> some of those shows can succeed on different levels,
> there's also the voyeuristic thrill, watching people being
> humiliated or brought to tears or suffering physically.
> And that's what I find very disturbing.

There's this potential for desensitizing the audience so
that when they see real tragedy playing out on the news,
it doesn't have the impact it should. It all just blurs into
one program. And I think it's very important not just for
young people, but for adults to make sure they're making
the distinction.

The producers had their own agenda, which was to make an entertaining show using the structure and language that had worked for
them for decades.

Unscripted television at its root plays to our most basic racist,
sexist, homophobic programming. It takes complex people and
makes them into sound bites, exploiting human emotions for ratings. When it's operating on all cylinders, it captures the suffering
of human existence. Even its artifice reflects our culture. But when
reality television is too real, it is no longer "so sad it is funny"; it is
just "so sad that viewers are complicit." Reality television is terrible. And I hate that I love it.

This is how I feel about my favorite show, *90 Day Fiancé*. The
premise is that couples apply for a special K-1 visa that gives them
ninety days together in the United States. They must decide in that
short amount of time whether they should get married and spend
the rest of their lives with each other, or break up (or, usually,
some messy combination of the two). Many of the couples who
met online, or on vacation at a resort, or via a mail-order bride ad,
struggle with the decision, as their prospective significant other is
always a total stranger to them. Still, in what is most likely to be
the worst decision of their lives, they go through with the union
because they are lonely, impoverished, or desperately want to

move to the United States of America for some reason. There is nothing that disrespects the institution of marriage[92] more than this TLC show and what feels like three hundred spinoffs.[93]

In what is by far the most xenophobic series on television, many Americans wield their passport like a weapon, intimidating their respective foreign spouses into submission. Razor-sharp editing captures the constant threat that if the immigrant doesn't behave,[94] they will have to go back to a "third world country." The racist interpersonal dynamics are intrinsic to the show's DNA. When we visit the foreign spouse's home country, we hear a score that feels like the sound designer searched "ethnic music" in the generic sound library. Meanwhile, the non-Americans on this show push the boundaries of what one would call a "loving relationship." Some barely hide their disdain for their partner. Others refuse to get a job. Many cheat. Every scene in *90 Day Fiancé* ends with me wishing that this couple would not have children together, only to find out in an upcoming scene that they are expecting.[95]

If you're interested in watching Angela, a bombastic blonde woman with leather skin from rural Georgia, bully Michael, an alleged Nigerian scammer with multiple cell phones, into having sex with her

---

92 In fact, someone should introduce the Westboro Baptist Church to this media property, as this is where they should be directing their ire as opposed to wedding cakes with two grooms on the top.

93 Spinoffs include *90 Day Fiancé: What Now?*, *The Family Chantel*, *90 Day Fiancé: Before the 90 Days*, *Darcey & Stacey*, *90 Day Fiancé: The Other Way*, *90 Day Fiancé: Self-Quarantined*, and my favorite, *90 Day Fiancé: Happily Ever After?* It is my favorite because as a Pisces I am a romantic at heart who wants things to end well. I enjoy seeing the ramifications of people's actions, because what is so stressful about the show is watching adults behave as if their actions do not have long-term consequences.

94 Read: as the American wants them to behave.

95 Congratulations!

or "going back to where he came from," this is the show for you. If you're interested in a convicted arsonist named Paul butcher his way through Portuguese and berate his kind, sweet pregnant wife, Karine, despite the fact that all he brings to the table is codependence on his aging mother and a lengthy prison record, this is the show for you. If you're interested in seeing Pedro's extended family break out into a fistfight in the Dominican Republic all because his partner, Chantel, mistook the word "puta," which loosely means "slut-whore," for "punto," which means "period," this is the show for you.

It was the show for me . . . until I met Darcey Silva at a press event. Darcey and her twin sister, Stacey, have had more televised break-ups than I've had real relationships. Unprompted, Silva expressed to me how happy she was . . . and that she was still a hopeless romantic . . . and that she was determined to find love . . . and that she had just joined an online dating community that connected singles with European men. . . . . . . I congratulated her. At that moment, I realized that my *fodder* was her *life*.

This is the precise dilemma of personality-driven reality television. Things get too real. This is most evident in season ten of *Vanderpump Rules*. The Bravo show captured national attention when Tom Sandoval cheated on his longtime partner, Ariana Madix, with her best friend, Raqual Leviss, the former fiancé of Tom's close friend James Kennedy. If this is hard to follow, understand that this incestual tomfoolery is a staple of the tenured show.

News of the drama, aptly referred to as Scandoval, broke playing out on the social media accounts of the castmates. As new episodes aired, viewers had the dramatic irony of knowing how the budding friendship between Ariana, Raquel, and Tom would end. Ariana started the season defending the often-questionable behavior of her best friend and boyfriend, only to realize the truth. These, in her words, were the worst people she ever met. It was a perfectly written tragedy . . . except, it was Ariana's reality.

While her personal life was gutted, Ariana benefited from public support. She landed a Lifetime movie, a slew of high-profile commercial endorsements, and the covers of fashion magazines. Meanwhile, Tom's restaurants, which had been documented on the show, suffered from negative reviews, slowed traffic, and pro-Ariana vandalism. Sandoval's stupid cover band was performing to empty crowds. I relished the hatred. I watched *Vanderpump Rules* for the cheating. These were not "great people," which is why they made great TV.

I felt vindicated watching bad people get exactly what they deserved. That was until I saw an article that said Raquel's parents had to contact the FBI because of violent and graphic death threats sent to multiple family members. Suddenly it wasn't just a show. It was real people's real lives being turned upside down by fans who took reality television seriously. I couldn't relate to acting on impulses to harass the very people who provided me with entertainment. I always approached the cast of reality shows as characters, my little Barbies who played on my screen. This gave me permission to say cruel things about them in my private group chats that I would never utter about real people in real life. But the public hatred directed at the latest cheaters in *Vanderpump Rules*'s long, storied history of cheaters reminded me that words have impacts. Suddenly, I pitied Raquel. Her character was evil. She slept with Ariana's boyfriend while she was away at her grandmother's funeral in ARIANA'S OWN HOME. She didn't deserve compassion. But . . . what if something bad happened?

As a spinoff, the series had already flirted with tragedy. In an early season of *Real Housewives of Beverly Hills*, Taylor Armstrong's husband, Russell, hung himself a month before the show's premiere. He had abused his wife for years, and the secret was revealed on the show in a group discussion at Lisa Vanderpump's house. This was a major storyline that fueled ratings and propelled *Real Housewives of Beverly Hills* to become one of the top shows on cable. This moment captures the danger looming over reality television. The stakes are always high. But where fiction allows observers to turn off the TV, this reality lives on- and off-screen, rippling in the castmates' lives for years or decades to come.

On the *Vanderpump* reunion episode, Ariana was asked what it was like during one of the most humiliating moments in her life to have the entire nation rallying behind her. Ariana began to sob, sharing that the support of her family and friends and fans kept her going. Then my perspective shifted. The issue isn't whether or not something bad might happen. Rather, it is how I can forget that the reason for our collective obsession with *Vanderpump Rules* is Ariana's misfortune. While her life seems better on the other side of these horrible friends, I can't forget that something bad happened . . . to her.

Of course, it was easy to lose sight of this when twenty minutes before, DJ James Kennedy aka the White Kanye West had referred to Sandoval as a "poopy head" and a "worm with a mustache."

lol

These are not serious people.

I hate that I love reality and I love to hate it.

I had my own agenda with the [REDACTED] dating show: Be nice, do not be sexist, make fun of the antiquated premise while respecting the institution. I got the women to cheer "marriage, marriage, marriage" like they were on *The Arsenio Hall Show*. I let my favorites win an obstacle course because the game was not *not* already fixed anyway. Knowingly or unknowingly, I was setting fire to drama, which is what excited me about the franchise in the first place. But where I itched to see Ashley A.[96] crying in a tankini because Jared "did not want to be with her," I was now trying to assuage nerves so the women did not feel alienated in their confessions about things like one-night stands and cheating history.

Later, after we wrapped shooting, I asked to take a group photo with the girls. I congratulated the winner and told her I was rooting for her (read: I did not *not* let her win). The girls told me that at first they thought I was scary and then realized I was actually *nice*. Slowly, I ingratiated into the sorority of sisterwives. I formed bonds that prompted some of them to confess that they loved one-night stands but their parents would be mad if they admitted that on television. They asked me if I had a YouTube channel. I said yes. And because they had no phones or computers during their incarceration at the dating-show mansion, they promised to check out my content when they had finished serving time.

That's when I remembered. We were all real people.

---

96   Ashley A. would go on to marry and have children with Jared, the man who rejected her on *Bachelor in Paradise* no fewer than four times, but this I suppose is a lesson in the persistence of women #imwithher.

damn.

Ziwe: *Is your country music a pivot, like when most musicians do rap and then they're like "I'm not black anymore" and then they do country?*

Chet Hanks: *I don't really have any plans. You know what I mean? I'm like the Joker. Do I look like a guy with a plan? I'm like a dog chasing cars, wouldn't know what to do if I got it! Batman, you complete me. My father was a drinker and a fiend. Yeah. RIP Heath. GOAT! They tried to kill my wife! Denzel.*

Ziwe: *Don't impersonate black men.*

Chet Hanks: *Shout out to John David Washington.*

Ziwe: *Do you ever feel like you're desecrating like black people when you do [BLEEP] like that?*

Chet Hanks: *Not at all.*

Ziwe: *Not at all. You feel like you're honoring them.*

Chet Hanks: *No, I don't feel like I'm doing anything. I feel like I'm just doing an impression.*

Ziwe: *Just being Chester Marlin Hanks.*

Chet Hanks: *LIVE IN THE FLESH. Haha, yeah. Yeah.*[97]

---

97 Excerpt from interview in *ZIWE* S2 E2, "Celebrity Rights Activist with Chet Hanks," May 8, 2022, on Showtime.

One time I auditioned to be a rotating host on a late-night variety show. It was like *The View* but with far less money and far more work. For six hours, the network held all of the prospective hosts captive in a windowless conference room while the Brett Kavanaugh confirmation hearings played in the background. The network insisted that we come up with "topical jokes" about the "sexual assault accusations" that the soon-to-be-Supreme-Court-justice was "crying about." Needless to say, it was a dark energy. We ate several meals in this 10 × 10 cell, and the room reeked of mayonnaise and salami because for some reason we were not allowed to leave. Over time, the executives called talent into a slightly larger windowless room to camera test with each other. I would not describe this as a pleasant auditioning experience, but sometimes you have to put up with questionable[98] conditions as a non-working working actor.

A mix of black and brown people auditioned for this job that ultimately all of us were too good for. Some were comedians, others were *New York Times* bestselling authors, and then there were the rappers. In this aboveground bunker, the rappers were the queen bees of the talent pool. The confidence! The sparkly jewelry! The unmitigated talent! Likely sharing my admiration, one blond actor was committed to befriending the rappers. The problem was that whenever he spoke to them, he made sure to lower his voice an octave and use words like "bling" and "fo sho" like a nonplayable character in *Grand Theft Auto*. I don't know whether this Westchester County thespian was consciously code-switching to connect with the rappers. However, the most alarming aspect of his performance of *What a White Man Thinks Black People Think Is Cool: The One*

---

98   Read: on the boundaries of what union and labor laws allow.

Man Show was that whenever he spoke to me, A BLACK WOMAN, he talked in his regular voice. The urban contemporary artists got the Lil Xan charm while I was left to hear his may-I-speak-to-the-manager voice. I am not exaggerating when I say the contrast in his tone was stark. To them he'd say, *"Word, I don't fuck with Fanta like dat, homies yo yo yo."* Only to follow with sentences to me like, *"Good day, dearest Ziwe, would you be so kind as to pass me some more prosciutto? I fancy cured meats. Indubitably."*

I think about this interaction every day.

Every.

Day.

There are few things as intimate as watching someone code-switch. I am just as perturbed by the racial implications of his blaccent as I am by the notion that he did not believe he had to use it on me. I have to assume that because I knew this actor, he was embarrassed that I could see through his performance. Still, to date, this is the only time in my life when I was insulted by not experiencing racism. I know I sound ridiculous, but you have to understand; the guy's sheer boldness in mumbling to rappers like a SoundCloud rapper and then in the very same breath dictating to me in the Queen's English left me vulnerable to the politics of my own blackness. Had private school stripped me of my authenticity? Or did this have nothing to do with me? Was this about the internal prejudice of Blaccent Guy? Or was I just wickety wickety wack?

In *The Souls of Black Folk*, W. E. B. Du Bois coined the term "double consciousness." This is the internal conflict that black Americans face as they struggle to move through the world as their truest selves while being aware of the external opinions of prejudiced onlookers. Thus, the challenge for a black person, especially in predominantly white institutions, comes from the need to conform to other people's perceptions of "normal" at the risk of not being able to assimilate. As we code-switch, we choose which portion of ourselves to reveal.

But at the heart of the debate around who gets to speak in AAVE (African American Vernacular English) is the idea that some people get to present *any* version of themselves, while others, in this case black people, are shamed for behavior that is seen as uneducated. We are forced to inhabit this double consciousness while other races performing blackness are free to express their creativity without reproach. A phrase like "It is giving periodt deadass slay" for some may just be a trendy expression of Gen Z slang.[99] But for others, like the black people[100] who pioneered this language decades ago, it serves as a reminder that their language is co-opted by people who do not resemble them, often for profit.

A great example of this is in the music industry: Macklemore won the Grammy Award for Best Rap Album at the 56th Annual Grammy Awards on January 26, 2014, beating out Kendrick Lamar's critically acclaimed album *good kid, m.A.A.d city*. Macklemore then posted on Instagram a text he sent Kendrick Lamar to apologize for this political upset.

---

99   Others could describe this phrase as successive terms illogically mashed together with no meaning. It is open for interpretation!

100   Specifically the queer black and brown community of the ballroom scene.

The blue text read,

> *You got robbed. I wanted you to win. You should have.*
> *It's weird and sucks that I robbed you. I was gonna say*
> *that during the speech. Then the music started playing*
> *during my speech and I froze. Anyway, you know what it*
> *is. Congrats on this year and your music. Appreciate you*
> *as an artist and friend. Much love.*

It's all very cringe. In my humble opinion, the Macklemore combination text-post is a crime that should be tried at the Hague. It's so performative to behave in a way that says "You deserve this and I'm gonna show how much you deserve this by posting our communications so everyone can see how good of a person I am." No judgment, right. I don't know this guy. I don't know how he's grown since this moment in time. But I can't stand this performance. It's bad enough that he gets rewarded for his derivative imitation. Even worse is that he feels guilty about it, but not enough for it to count. Either shut up and take the money or don't participate at all. But the middle ground of awareness is an insult wrapped in a bow. If you're going to be problematic, say it with your chest.

Four years later, Kendrick Lamar would go on to win a Pulitzer Prize for his album *DAMN*. Though this lesson on the arbiters of culture remains, a win is a win.

My parents speak several languages and I speak only one, maybe 1.5 if you count how fluent I am in Spanish when I am *borracha*. Their reason for not teaching their children their native tongue was fear that if people heard us speaking a language other than English they would discriminate against us. It is one of my life's disappointments that I am not fluent in Igbo or Yoruba. These languages would connect me more closely to my parents' culture in addition to making me a worldlier person (and a more competitive job applicant). But my parents were not inherently wrong, as I watched firsthand how people would discriminate against *them* just because they spoke with an accent.

The way I speak has always been an amalgamation of my different environments. If I spend a lot of time with my parents, strangers will say I sound like I have a British accent. If I spend time with my childhood friends, I'll settle into AAVE, and if I am with my friends from private school, I will unconsciously channel my best impression of *The Fresh Prince of Bel Air*'s Hilary Banks. All of these interpretations of language make it easier to move from predominantly black spaces to predominantly white spaces to everything in between. But in my double consciousness, I am hyperaware of the policing of onlookers who at any given time may think I speak too properly or not properly enough.[101]

The truth is, I am filled with disdain when non-black people drop black slang in my direction. I don't think it's fair. Of course, people should be allowed to enjoy food and clothes and music from other cultures without indictment. But what's the difference between appreciation and appropriation? It's sort of like pornography: You know it when you see it. And in that case, Cody Rigsby's Peloton[102]

---

101   Read: ghetto, hood . . . although these words contradict each other, as the vernacular of American ghettos can now be heard in every wealthy suburb with a Spotify account.

102   I got a Peloton three months into the pandemic because I had a sudden realization that the whole "quarantine" thing was not going to end anytime soon. During the early months, I had probably taken about thirty steps collectively. Heart disease is real and thus, in the words of Michelle Obama, I needed to "let's move."

class is my favorite porn.[103] As a self-described "white gay," Rigsby has the interesting habit of speaking in AAVE throughout his rides. It is equal parts laughable and maddening. Unlike his peer instructors, like Tunde and Ally Love, who I have noticed make a habit of keeping their language clean of profanity, Cody Rigsby is not afraid to call you a *bitch* (positively and negatively) or a *yas queen*, or to threaten to *"drag the workout by its edges"* (???), an analogy he uses often.

Do not get me wrong; Cody Rigsby has wonderful playlists including bops from Ariana Grande, Megan Thee Stallion, and our mutual hero, Britney Spears. What "inspires" me most about this Peloton instructor, which I realize is a wild sentence to type out, is that Cody often twerks during the hard parts of the workout while he encourages me to pedal harder. So he'll say something like, "Okay, turn your resistance to seventy and your cadence to one hundred," and then he will just start body rolling as I pedal uphill. It's common courtesy that if I am expected to lose my breath, he could at least be there in the trenches with me. But he chooses not to, which is part of his power. Instead, Cody makes sassy vocalizations while I fight for my life. During this process, I permit myself to pick apart everything about him that I don't like for a forty-five-minute uphill climb that ends with a Diana Ross × Skrillex dubstep remix.

---

103   Since the publishing of this book, I have sold my Peloton to a friend's mom for 70 percent of its original value, because it was a terrible coatrack. By all definitions, buying a Peloton when I am not a person who "enjoys" "working out" was a bad business decision. My friend's mom doesn't use it either. We both regret the purchase.

All of this would be infuriating, but Cody is entertaining in his manic hyperbole. He covers a wide breadth of irrelevant topics over the course of his workouts that are a distracting fever dream of dissociative episodes. Here is a real Cody Rigsby transcript of a soliloquy about Angelica Pickles from the 1990s Nickelodeon cartoon *Rugrats*:

> *If I was little Tommy Pickles . . . or little Chuckie . . .*
> *or Phil and Lil . . . Angelica would have caught these*
> *hands . . . Okay! . . . she would have left daycare with a*
> *black eye.*

> *She was bossy, and rude, and Phil and Lil and Tommy*
> *and Chuckie, they did not deserve all that energy. Okay!*
> *She did not deserve . . . they did not deserve all that*
> *energy.*

> *Chill out, Angelica! Uh-uh, gurl, you too mean . . . Get out*
> *my face . . . Uh-uh, just 'cause you're one year and three*
> *months older than me . . . ? No, ma'am, get out of here.*

> *Take your raggedy ass little doll too. You crazy, Angelica.*
> *You pulled out her hair and stuff . . . ? Uh-uh, you ain't the*
> *boss of me.*

This is a grown man directing ire at a children's television show that has been *off the air* for almost twenty years. While the politics of advocating for cartoon babies to beat a cartoon toddler's ass are . . . absurd, it's worth pointing out that this rant has absolutely nothing to do with cycling. And what the transcript does not capture is Cody Rigsby's interspersed hand gestures, head movements, lip smacks, and palate clicks, which would indicate to any cultured rider of the $3,000 bike that he definitely has four to five black friends.

Yet, I exclusively take his classes because he is the only instructor who knows how to reach me where I am with the motivators I need. I sprint faster because his words invigorate me. Other instructors talk about working out for *the individual in the mirror*, competing against yourself to achieve personal goals irrespective of external expectations. This allows you to define what winning means for you. I appreciate that idealism, but at this moment neither of my selves can relate. How do you win for yourself when the world constantly moves the goalpost? You can't. At least not at their game. That makes me just mad enough to get over that hill. A win is a win.

imposter syndrome

Ziwe: Welcome. I'm your host, Ziwe, and, much like Naomi Campbell, I am a model minority. It's not easy being a minority in America, and I'm going to make it harder by pitting myself against an Asian woman. Please welcome Aparna Nancherla.

Aparna: Hi. Ziwe.

Ziwe: Are Indians the black people of Asians?

Aparna: You want a sound bite.

Ziwe: Yeah, I want a sound bite.

Aparna: Do you want me to say Indian people are the black people of Asians?

Ziwe: Please, just to camera.

Aparna: I can't.

Ziwe: No?

Aparna: I can't say it.

Ziwe: Wow, okay.

Aparna: I mean, I did. I was hoping you caught it then.

Ziwe: Okay well we'll just—we'll recut that. Editing is magic.

Aparna: Okay.

Ziwe: *Editing is magic.*

Aparna: *Okay.*

Ziwe: *Editing editing is mag-mag-magic!*

Aparna [poorly edited to say horrible things that Aparna would never say]: *I hate Indian people, Filipino people, Indian people, white women, Blasians, model minorities, science, some of your Eastern Asians, Indian and African immigrant parents, black people. I love racism!*[104]

People always ask me who my favorite guest is. Choosing a favorite guest is like naming a favorite child.[105] I've spoken to political icons like Gloria Steinem and Stacey Abrams, cultural lightning rods like Julia Fox, Mia Khalifa, and Chet Hanks, acclaimed comedians like Nicole Byer and Bowen Yang, and brilliant drag queens like Katya Zamolodchikova and Bob the Drag Queen. All of them are iconic guests.

What makes an icon exactly? "Iconic" is an overused word in the English lexicon. This adjective is used to describe "looks" and "clapbacks" and "relationship goals" in a way that makes the word devoid of any real meaning. From my perspective, "iconic" simply means that something is memorable, and whether it be pejorative or appreciative, I let my audience make that judgment. After all, iconic is in the eye of the beholder.[106]

---

104   Excerpt from interview with Aparna Nancherla, "Model Minorities," February 5, 2020, on Instagram Live.

105   Every parent has one, but it would be a mistake to tell the children that.

106   Or is it . . .

For many, Martin Luther King Jr. is a civil rights icon. This is sort of an indisputable fact to anyone who is not a racist hater. But, to some, Robert E. Lee is an icon. And while Robert E. Lee is a hero only to a relatively small subset of humanity, I share this to establish that the word "icon" does not discriminate between one of the greatest orators in American history and an ugly traitorous Confederate general who could not win a civil war if his life depended on it. Iconic guests come in all shapes and sizes, and the only requirement is that they stimulate discourse.

I don't have a favorite guest, but my interview with Aparna Nancherla cemented the genre. She is one of the funniest people in comedy, and *my goodness* is that woman smart and not racist. Usually, this is a good quality, but for entertainment purposes it's quite difficult to establish a game based on racial faux pas when the other player is an inoffensive person. After I finished taping, I was stressed about how this episode that played against the show's entire premise would work. But that's the magic of editing, which became an inside joke as I regularly declared "editing is magic" before intentionally misquoting Aparna in bad faith.

This is the art of my interview style: "baited," coined after the term "race baiter," an accusation that Fox News would "occasionally" hurl at President Barack Obama for doing controversial things like being black and talking about the fact that he was black. This impossible line of questioning lends itself to jumping to wild conclusions, putting words in people's mouths, and not listening. All things I would consider hilarious, if they weren't so damaging to the democracy. Every question is predicated on the ideology that no matter what the interview subject says, the interviewer will find a way to spin it to favor their biases. It is not meant to extrapolate news or factual information, but rather act as a cultural litmus test for audience members. I would liken it to a persistent grandma guilt-tripping her grandchild into eating her delicious homemade cooking and then immediately turning around to call that grandchild chubby as she force-feeds them pork sausage. But in this case, all the grandchildren get canceled.

I shot the first iteration of this interview on November 9, 2016, the day after Hillary Clinton's least-favorite Election Day. It was a major historical event. Aparna's interview aired in February 2020.

My overnight success, which had been ten years in the making, started with a global pandemic. I did not know it at the time, but March 19 would be the last day I attended a live *Desus & Mero* taping as an employee. In the blink of our eyes, every New Yorker, save for the underpaid and overworked essential workers, was confined to their home for an indefinite amount of time.

As the city worked to avoid one disease, we collectively came down with another: cabin fever. This resulted in what I would describe as a "very weird time" in American history. Some of us made celebrities out of accused murderers/tiger enthusiasts; others began bread-making, searching for meaning in the dough they kneaded; and far too many went live on Instagram at every waking hour of the day.

I was one of those people. My community of comedians continued the live shows they put on hold virtually. I did not want to be left behind, so I tried a variety of formats before landing on an interview show where I asked people uncomfortable questions about race. It would be a new iteration of my YouTube show *Baited with*

Ziwe, which had a cult following among pockets of people but at the time had not achieved mainstream success.

On April 9, 2020, I interviewed my first guests for my Instagram Live show. These early episodes were very low in audience attendance. For a performer, there is nothing more humiliating than performing to an empty crowd. Except in my case, it was to an Instagram audience of maybe thirty people, when I knew for a fact that every single person in my life was home and most definitely on their phone.

As an artist you can be doing what you think is radical, thoughtful, good work, but sometimes people do not show up. It is not because you are not talented; it is because others do not care. Sometimes your supply does not align with the universe's demand. This is basic economics. It calls to mind something Cardi B once said about stripping that has always stuck with me. The reality-television-star-turned-chart-topping-rapper once said, "It is not fun and games. Everyone always asks me, 'What's the most you made in a strip club?' I'll say the most I ever did was seven thousand in one night. And some girls is like, 'What's the least you make?' And girls will say, 'Oh, I'd say about five hundred.' No! The least you ever made is nothing! Zero dollars! Nada! Some girls are afraid to say that, afraid to let people know they take Ls, they suffer casualties."

Performing live emotionally prepared me to look failure in the eye without blinking. Because failure happens most of the time. After years of no one caring about my work, a valuable lesson I learned from rejection is that I cannot live my life for external validation. This seems contradictory, because most artwork directly prompts the validation of applause or laughter or furrowed brows and nodding heads. But external validation is a bottomless pit—there's no amount that'll make you feel whole if you do not love yourself. So I resolved, much later than I would have liked to, to create to entertain myself.

My earliest interviews were both wildly spellbinding and highly problematic. In producing a show that was live and public, I had run into a very obvious yet unforeseen issue: I could not stop my guests from saying offensive things, especially after baiting them into saying offensive things.

There is no editing with the Instagram Live format. This is part of its appeal. Viewers get to watch my guest and me think in real time, observing conversations unfold like a slow-motion car crash. In the post–Fyre Festival world, where internet users had become distrustful of the manicured curation of social media, my show was *too* real, painfully real, reminiscent of the sensational spontaneity of live television.

Every Thursday at 8:00 P.M. EST, I interviewed a myriad of guests, including Jes Tom, Benito Skinner, Sarah Sherman, Rachel Sennott, Jordan Mendoza, Cole Escola, and Bradford Evans. Before the show blew up, none of these guests were the publicly canceled or problematic individuals the show would go on to be known for. The show was just a funny forum to discuss race with other comedians I followed on Instagram.

As the show's audience grew, I looked to expand my guest pool beyond "acquaintances who would respond to my direct messages." I worked for months to book Caroline Calloway. I had first become familiar with Calloway when she went viral on Twitter for hosting an influencer retreat priced at $176.68 per person, as chronicled by a critic, Kayleigh Donaldson. Tickets for the retreat were sold in Boston, Denver, San Francisco, Los Angeles, Atlanta, Chicago, Dallas, Austin, Charlotte, and DC, before Caroline had allegedly ever booked the venues. Donaldson described it as the Fyre Festival of Seminars, centered on Calloway teaching people how to "be themselves." Chaos arose when Calloway was exhausted from making salads so she invited her fans to bring their own lunches, despite the inclusion of a guaranteed vegan lunch in the ticket pricing. She also may have invited her Boston and Philadelphia fans to travel to a New York venue because it was "better." However, my favorite detail was the allegation that her "orchid crowns" were made of one (1) single flower—therefore not qualifying as a crown. Everything about this event was iconic to me.

One day, absolutely out of the blue, Caroline Calloway followed me on Instagram. I had not tweeted about her or tagged her. This felt random. Perhaps an act of God? I DMed her asking if she would ever consider being on my show. I waited thirty minutes, no response. I started to spiral, as I am wont to do. I was surprised when later that day Caroline Calloway expressed interest but respectfully declined.

I considered Caroline Calloway's pass as an opening and waited a couple of weeks and then asked her again. Still no. Everything I knew about booking my Instagram Live show I learned from striking out as a live performer/producer in New York. Of course, no means no. Unless it is in regard to talent booking—then "no" means "maybe definitely probably sometime in the future after the show has become more popular." I knew that Caroline Calloway was a key figure in my interview show's pop-culture breakthrough.

I was playing the long game.

Then, on May 26, the national protests erupted. Several news outlets characterized this moment of externalized grief as "violent protests" and "looting." I guess they weren't protesting, right? Decades earlier, in an interview for *Esquire* magazine, James Baldwin was asked how he would define looting following the assination of Martin Luther King Jr.:

> *Before I get to that, how would you define somebody*
> *who puts a cat where he is and takes all the money out*
> *of the ghetto where he makes it? Who is looting whom?*
> *Grabbing off the TV set? He does not really want the*
> *TV set. He's saying screw you. It is just judgment, by*
> *the way, on the value of the TV set. He does not want*
> *it. He wants to let you know he's there. The question*
> *I am trying to raise is a very serious question. The*
> *mass media-television and all the major news agencies*
> *endlessly use that word "looter." On television you*
> *always see black hands reaching in, you know. And*
> *so the American public concludes that these savages*
> *are trying to steal everything from us. And no one has*
> *seriously tried to get where the trouble is. After all,*
> *you're accusing a captive population who has been*
> *robbed of everything of looting. I think it is obscene.*
> —James Baldwin, Esquire, *July 1968*

George Floyd's tragic murder marked a watershed moment. We were living through another major historical event as millions of Americans seemed to wake up from the fantasy that we lived in a post-racial society. And with life as we know it on indefinite hiatus, all we had was free time. Time to reflect. Time to mourn. Time to mobilize. Thus, the question wasn't why are black Americans looting? Or why are black Americans so angry? The question was: What did we expect would happen when people were left to sit with their thoughts and realize exactly how bad things were?

These protests opened the floodgates of cultural reckoning. People started examining themselves, prompting uncomfortable conversations about a usually taboo subject: race. Finally, my art aligned with the universe. And I couldn't have been more depressed. I didn't really see the point of doing anything, least of all making comedy. A friend encouraged me to express this despondence in my work. Just be me.

For the third time, I asked Caroline Calloway if she would be interested in an interview on my Instagram Live show, because I thought she'd be an iconic guest. This time, Caroline Calloway agreed, becoming the first influencer I ever interviewed. Where Aparna inspired post-truth editorial, Calloway set the standard for performing allyship.

> **Ziwe:** *Now, first question for you, Caroline, is I watched your Cambridge Union interview today, and you said that famously you discovered racism in 2018. What were you doing for the first twenty-five years of your life?*
>
> **Caroline Calloway:** *I didn't say I discovered it like Christopher Columbus discovered America. I said, I was careful to say I began my journey with racism in 2018, and honestly I was fucking around for the first twenty-five years of my life. I was literally such a dumb white girl. I would shudder to think if you could have twenty-five-year-old Caroline on the show. It would, it would not be funny.*

Ziwe: *I see.*|

Caroline Calloway: *It would be awful.*

Ziwe: *And what in 2018 after twenty-five years of life woke you up to the fact that racism was a problem that existed?*

Caroline Calloway: *Honestly, um, I started following women online like Rachel Cargle, like Leyla Saad, and just learning about the fact that like the women who I had idolized like Susan B. Anthony like these sort of like incredible monumental figures of white feminism when I started seeing that they had actively spoken out against black people. That they had spoken in favor of the superiority of the white race. I was like, holy shit, everything I know is a lie, and that, you know, the women's rights movement and the civil rights movement didn't go as far as I thought it did.*

Ziwe: *Wow. I really appreciate that thoughtful answer. Now I saw on your Instagram that you are promoting black authors, like Wesley Lowery, who wrote* They Can't Kill Us, *and* The New Jim Crow *by Michelle Alexander.*

Caroline Calloway: *Austin Channing, let's fucking go. Layla Saad . . .*

Ziwe: *Exactly.*

Caroline Calloway: *Let's go!*

Ziwe: *Now you're a vociferous reader, how many of these books have you read?*

Caroline Calloway: *Honestly, of the nine books that I recommended on my Instagram I've read four.*

Ziwe: *Wow.*

Caroline Calloway: *But I've ordered the other five from black bookshops, so I would like my ally cookie now.*

Ziwe: *There are no cookies in this game. Now can you tell me who Marcus Garvey is?*

Caroline Calloway: *Never heard of him.*

Ziwe: *Never heard of him. Okay, interesting. What about Huey P. Newton?*

Caroline Calloway: *Is he a poet of the Harlem Renaissance? Because otherwise, I don't know him.*

Ziwe: *Absolutely not.*

Caroline Calloway: *Okay, cool.*

Ziwe: *Fred Hampton?*

Caroline Calloway: *I don't know any of these names.*

Ziwe: *Angela Davis?*

Caroline Calloway: *Angela Davis is a civil rights activist. Who is still alive, and it's weird to me that we're not listening to her more? Like why are we listening to like, I don't know like Glennon Doyle and Reese Witherspoon talk about activism when Angela Davis is literally still alive. Like it's so weird to me.*

Here I was interviewing Calloway on the complex topic of race in America. Like in a WWE fight, we entered the ring and performed our perspectives as the audience cheered for the hero and the heel. It was a spectacle. Overnight, I blew up, positioned as the Ellen DeGeneres of race relations, where if people did something problematic, or iconic, as my viewers described, culprits would have to come to my principal's office and seek penance. The truth is that not only did I not want the power to absolve anyone, but I didn't have it. My work was never that serious. I was just a comedian who happened to be at the right place at the right time. Four months prior, I was wondering what show I would get staffed on next. Now I found myself fielding offers.

I knew that I was ready. I had been hustling for years, and opportunity finally met my preparation. But I couldn't shake the fear that I was an imposter. Everything could fall apart if I wasn't perfect.

I didn't realize this was an insecurity of mine until recently when I was honored with my own ranking on the inaugural *Forbes* Top Creators list of 2022. I had many aversions to this public acknowledgment, a privilege I fought tooth and nail, as evidenced by the following email I sent to my publicists.

> SUBJECT LINE: RE: Ziwe: FORBES Top Creators List
>
> thanks for the help
>
> I would not like to be on this list
>
> I would not describe myself as an influencer or creator as I do not post original content[107] on social media and I frequently deactivate my twitter
>
> If anything I am a moderately successful writer actor and television host which means I am at the bottom of *Forbes* Hollywood as opposed to *Forbes* influencer

I was half kidding.

It's not that I didn't appreciate this distinction; it's that I didn't feel it was appropriate. How could I be a top influencer when I did not identify as one at all? To me, influencers were people who shared

---

107   This is not even true. I do post original content on social media. That is literally my job.

pictures of themselves on perpetual vacation flaunting their thigh gaps and #blessed #ad designer bags. They were the Instagram accounts with 30 million followers that reposted screenshots of other people's jokes without attribution. They were the useless protagonists in *Triangle of Sadness* who in a shipwreck scenario offered nothing but snide commentary. Despite my antipathy for the words, I started my professional career like most young people: on the internet. It just so happens that my content creation ran parallel to my corporate development as a writer. I did not feel like an influencer. Sure, I posted original content to my social media accounts, but they were curated interviews directed to my niche online following. Sure, I shared sponsored posts, but only because money.[108] Sure, I attended an influencer screening of *Ingrid Goes West*, a movie about the pathologies of influencer culture, but only because I love watching movies for free.[109]

Now—even as I type this—I realize that the lady doth protest too much. "Influencer" and "creator" were very accurate characterizations of the lane I had found for myself, and I was good at it. While I was working as an unpaid intern, then as a barbecue hostess, then as a writing assistant, then as a writer, I was moonlighting as an internet personality. I was "content creating" to circumvent any gatekeeping that would preclude me, a young black woman without famous parents, from entering the industry. I leveraged my digital audience to get creative jobs and then I leveraged those creative jobs to build my audience. Yet I could not visualize myself

---

108   mostly*******

109   *Ingrid Goes West* is the story of Ingrid (Aubrey Plaza), who moves to Los Angeles and stalks and befriends fictional influencer Taylor Sloane (Elizabeth Olsen), falsifying her entire life story. Over the course of the film, Taylor discovers Ingrid's lies and excommunicates her from the friend group. This prompts Ingrid to livestream her attempted suicide, which goes viral, ultimately making Ingrid internet famous.

OKAY WE INTERRUPT THIS STORY FOR A BRIEF ESSAY ON MY AWAKENING

My own racial awakening had come seven years earlier, with Trayvon Martin's murder at the hands of George Zimmerman and the subsequent 2013 trial. I was interning at *The Colbert Report* the week the trial verdict was announced. I was young, so I had faith that the justice system would provide justice. I suppose decades of watching Detectives Benson and Stabler arrest, prosecute, and imprison sexual predators in a record sixty minutes including commercial breaks had fooled me into believing that justice was always served.

What shows like *Law & Order: SVU*, *Paw Patrol*, *Inspector Gadget*, and *Chip 'n' Dale: Rescue Rangers* fail to include is that often policing assumes guilty until proven innocent for everyone but a "select" "few." This often leaves people dead or maimed before they are ever able to state their case. Unsurprisingly, extrajudicial murders do not make good fodder for Saturday-morning cartoons. So, many people believe in the intrinsic justice of the justice system, because that is what we have seen on television for the majority of our lives. We have been socialized to believe everything works as it should.

Nothing shocked me like Trayvon Martin. I believed that a grown man ignoring direct orders from a 911 dispatcher about pursuing a teenager in a hoodie and then killing him in cold blood would obviously, most certainly be against the law.

I was a junior in college at the time and I had a lot to learn about the world.

History tells us that George Zimmerman was acquitted of all wrongdoing, in part because his lawyers used the Stand Your Ground law as his defense. This law specified that people may use deadly force when they reasonably believe it to be necessary to defend against a threat of death, serious bodily harm, kidnapping, rape, and so on. Logic would make even the most reasonable person question how George Zimmerman could claim "stand your ground" when he allegedly stalked a seventeen-year-old. But with time I have learned that "logic" is not what makes the world turn. And in this case, a certain "logic" was exploited with the jurors as Martin was tried in the media. During this trial, the public learned that Trayvon Martin had been suspended from school at the time of his death, with CNN reporting that his suspension was due to marijuana possession. Photos circulated of Trayvon in removable gold grills and a hoodie, holding his middle finger up to the camera, while his Twitter and

Facebook revealed his hatred of school and love of DMX. Photos circulated from Martin's social media that depicted the teenager as violent and menacing, even though, I should reiterate, he was a victim. He died with only an AriZona Iced Tea and a bag of Skittles in his pockets. As has been the case with so many black boys after him, Trayvon Martin stood trial for his own death in the media. This was a system that assumed him guilty until proven innocent.

This trial triggered a debate on Twitter, a website not known for its nuanced discourse. Twitter is a horrible place that should not exist. At worst, it is a website that allows extremists to disseminate misinformation that compromises democratic elections across the globe. In its defense, most social media sites do that . . . rhymes with Facebook. At best, Twitter is a website that offers dank memes and a space for people to connect and amplify their voices. And because it is a website that publicizes people's opinions, I could see the incredibly bad takes from former classmates, friends, strangers, politicians, bots, and favorite (and not-so-favorite) celebrities.

This is the problem with social media. The human brain is not meant to interact with this many people's opinions on any given day. I am not saying globalization is bad, but . . . points were made. It is not useful to know what the girl from my freshman sociology class who liked to chew with her mouth open thought about the Thirteenth Amendment. Under normal circumstances, this person would fade from my consciousness. But in the interconnected world of Twitter and Facebook and LinkedIn, I was doomed to remember that the people I disliked years ago could still give me new, profound reasons to dislike them in the present day.

So many people I followed had no reservations about publicly opining about respecting the justice system's decision to exonerate George Zimmerman. And even worse, many of them disagreed with me. Trayvon Martin had become one of the first viral lynching stories of the social media era. If Zimmerman's acquittal bamboozled me, the disconnect between my peers' interpretation of the trial and mine broke my heart. Suddenly, I saw the world differently. And just like that, I was awake.

on any *Forbes* list that features an alarming number of entrepreneurs accused of financial crimes.

THIS IS NOT AN INDICTMENT OF THE *FORBES* LIST. THIS IS AN INDICTMENT OF LISTS.

Let's take Sam Bankman-Fried, the wunderkind and CEO of cryptocurrency exchange FTX. In 2022, SBF covered the vaunted *Forbes* 400. That same year FTX was forced to file for bankruptcy after a run of customers withdrew an estimated $6 billion over the course of seventy-two hours, dropping his net worth 94% overnight. Soon, news accused Bankman-Fried of using billions of dollars in customer funds to cover losses and make bets in Alameda, the hedge fund managed by a woman he was allegedly sleeping with. Allegedly! He was later hit with twelve criminal charges, including fraud and conspiracy, to which he pled not guilty. Fun fact: Sam Bankman-Fried and I were in the same class of *Forbes*'s 30 Under 30, in Finance and Entertainment respectively. Did he experience imposter syndrome like me? Or was he always confident that he'd change the world? He once played League of Legends while pitching an investor for hundreds of millions of dollars, so I must assume the latter.

Let's take the CEO of Theranos, Elizabeth Holmes. Her company dared to dream of cutting-edge technology that ran more than thirty lab tests using only one drop of blood. Over time, the company adjusted its promises to technology that runs "dozens of lab tests" using "a few drops of blood." Eventually, the public learned that not only did Theranos's futuristic blood testing not exist, but it was often wrong—once misdiagnosing a patient with HIV. But, before the Justice Department sentenced her to federal prison for defrauding investors, Elizabeth Holmes was crowned the youngest female self-made billionaire on the cover of the *Forbes* 400 issue.

There was also Charlie Javice, the founder and former CEO of Frank, a student financial aid application assistance company that she described as "the Amazon of higher education." In her company's $175 million sale to J.P. Morgan, Javice allegedly claimed she had four million users and then paid an "outside data scientist" $18,000 to create a fake customer list. The US Justice Department noted Javice's inclusion in the 2019 *Forbes* 30 Under 30 list in the same press release that announced charges of conspiracy, wire fraud, bank fraud, and securities fraud filed against her.

Who gets to be an imposter? A couple of days ago I woke up in the middle of the night with what I thought was a genius idea. I began furiously typing on my phone, "a cost-effective subscription service that allows people to read as many books as possible while cutting down on the environmental waste of printing books." The next morning, I was disappointed to discover that the life-changing idea that had stirred me from my slumber was actually just . . . a library. But under the right circumstances, could I have made the next Uber for Books? The answer is no. I am jealous of the Elizabeth Holmeses, Sam Bankman-Frieds, and Charlie Javices of the world. There seems to be serenity in being able to lie to the world at a scale that values your lies at a billion dollars. I can barely convince myself that I am worth half the hype.

I have always been deeply triggered by lists. My parents survived genocide—if anything, family history has taught me that it is rarely a good thing to be on a list. The issue with lists is that they breed discontent. When I was left off lists like "The 50 Funniest Arbitrary People in Williamsburg That You Should Know and Anyone Not On the List Is a Loser Who Should Die Alone," I felt like all my hard work was a waste of time. Like no one noticed me, or even worse, they saw me but did not actually care. As I had always suspected, I was screaming into the void.

A publication did a roundup of the one hundred funniest, most influential comedy figures on the internet of the 2010s. It felt like every one of my peers was on the list but me. I cried myself to sleep and made it my New Year's resolution to be on more lists in 2020. This was my second-most-embarrassing New Year's resolution after "Learn to do an adult backflip." (A backflip is something that I believe I am too old to do without a high risk of breaking my neck. My favorite thing about my New Year's resolutions is that they always seem trivial with time. I would soon learn that lists would be the least of my concerns as I spent 2020 in a hermetically sealed bubble with little exposure to sunlight.) I wanted so desperately to be acknowledged, validated, because this meant that all of my work was worth the blood, sweat, and tears, which is my dramatic description of sitting on an aerodynamic swivel chair and typing.

For a lot of people, the risk of failure is enough to stop them from ever pursuing their true passion. I have a disgusting obsession with perfection. I don't feel I have the same margins for error as others. I wish I could say this was all in my head, but the expression "You have to work twice as hard to be half as good" didn't just fall from the sky. I'm rewriting this essay in the eleventh hour because I can't escape the thought that if every expression is not acutely articulated then people will know that I am imperfect.

For that reason, I am never satisfied. I like to think that my goal-oriented nature gives me my drive. But really, it's an addiction. The problem with the gold apple is that it has seeds; success is an endless pursuit.

In a televised conversation, Maya Angelou once asked the famed writer, "How do you cope with success? And after that—if you want to weave them together it is fine with me—how do you cope with despair? Despair in front of the fact that the world is saying you're a success. Okay, so—okay?"

> **James Baldwin:** *I think but I don't know. Well, in my own case, you know, in a paradoxical fashion, which you cannot possibly*

explain, what is called success in my own case, right, came out of despair.

Maya Angelou: *No, of course. Of course, life out of death, death out of life.*

James Baldwin: *That's how you learn to live with despair. You live with despair. Success, I must say, is a little like finding yourself on a runaway horse, because you never see it coming, and also, in a very serious way, it is not possible, it is not possible, for an artist to be a success. You know?*

Maya Angelou: *Would you say that again?*

James Baldwin: *I said it is not possible for an artist to be a success.*

Maya Angelou: *Thank you.*

James Baldwin: *Once you think of yourself as a success . . .*

Maya Angelou: *You're finished. Finito.*

James Baldwin: *Forget it.*

Maya Angelou: *You know what I find is that you begin to believe your own publicity.*

James Baldwin: *You begin to take your identity from other people—*

Maya Angelou: *—from somebody else, and you stop experimenting because somebody says well when you did so-and-so, that was such a success, why don't you do that again?*

People ask me how and why I am so confident in the work that I do. I am not. I maintain confidence by searching within. With everything that I create, my question is always: Why am I doing this? Is it for money? Is it for attention? Is it to help people? Is it to heal myself? Is it because if I am anything less than perfect, I feel I do not deserve love? Making myself not only have clear intentions but articulate them provides me with a rubric upon which to judge my work. Knowing my own intentions allows me to judge my work. I can't control whether others think I'm worthy. Some people think Robert E. Lee is an icon.

My art is not about success. My art is about me—my life, my experiences, my perspective. *That* is my cheat code. I remind myself that I am one of a kind. I am special. I have something to say. And even if no one cares, I do. The only way I could be an imposter is if I'm not true to myself.

adopt don't shop

I've been trying to adopt a dog for the past nine months. Despite submitting several applications all over the Greater New York area, not one (1) rescue shelter has reached out to me about placing a pooch in my home. Before you grow critical of what—according to these organizations—appears to be my lack of "qualifications" for "keeping an animal alive," please recognize that I am not applying for puppies. In fact, I do not want an adolescent coming into my apartment and peeing on my cream-colored carpets or chewing my Manolo Blahniks. Nay. I am looking to adopt a later-in-life lapdog, a geriatric gal who's been cast aside by society, much like myself as I approach the rotten age of [REDACTED].

I love older dogs, mostly because they act like felines without the incessant "meowing." No disrespect to cat people, as I do identify as an indoor cat—emotionally withholding, vindictive, and a lover of tuna.

Yet despite my work-from-home status, burgeoning career, and willingness to support senior-citizen canines, my phone line has been dead when it should be ringing with opportunities for me to be a good person and *Adopt Don't Shop*™.

Now, I am not one to criticize a social/political movement, but this is a major flaw in the *Adopt Don't Shop*™ ideology. Few take into consideration how easy and effortless *Shop Don't Adopt*™ is. And while I would never ever fall into temptation for fear of public backlash and the wrath of PETA, surely going to a breeder for immediate gratification has its benefits. Rather, I am stuck combing through PetFinder looking for breeds that match my personality and applying for the privilege of having a lazy freeloader live under my roof. This is a task I do without complaint, in spite of the labor-intensive process of presenting recommendations, my lease contract, and comprehensive essays about why I deserve to have unconditional love in my life, only to be met with radio silence! . . . Does it sound like I'm bitter? I am not! This is just the emotional diatribe of someone without an emotional support animal.

Still, I recognize that animal shelters are doing their absolute best. During the pandemic, they received an influx of applications from unqualified prospective owners. Kennels are perhaps more hesitant about matching animals that they cannot guarantee will have a safe household.

But I am not those people. I am just as deserving as the 23 million American households that got pets during the pandemic. I am a wonderful creature enthusiast.[110] I have a host of dog trainer

---

110   Recently, I have taken to scooping frogs that get stuck in the pool of the Airbnb I am staying at to write this book. Do they want to get into my pool skimmer? Unsure. Have I mistakenly flung a few into the sky in a state of panic? That's not something I would admit to in print. Still, I have rescued more than twenty-four frogs over the course of two weeks. Yet no one appreciates

friends in my life because while, again, I identify as a cat, I surround myself with dog people. And more importantly I am famous. So . . . give me what I want, which, at this exact moment, is to have a pet!!!!

I am not trying to point fingers here, but I have seen a lot of people posting their new dogs this year and I would be remiss if I didn't ask the important questions. Has anyone looked into the statistical patterns of who animal shelters allow to adopt? I would like to see a comprehensive long-form study on racism in the dog adoption process. Over the course of this fruitless process, I have had to fill out a number of fields, including things like my name, marital status (?!), and experience with owning dogs, which on the surface seem harmless but upon closer examination offer opportunities for discrimination. Where is the race-blind admissions commission? Would I have a dog if my name were John Smith and I were married to a heterosexual woman? Who is to say but the ASPCA? All I know is that people have been owning animals for millennia without the red tape of sharing personal details like "Do you have loved ones?" If we can believe that racism is institutionalized across all branches of American industry, then we have to give long consideration to the implicit bias in not giving me a dog that I need because I am sad. Where is the nation's first black attorney general, Eric Holder, when you need him?

the painstaking steps I am taking tow
about my rescue missions, she resp
sorry you have to deal with all thos‹
safety of those amphibians that get
as opposed to a chlorinated grave. I
accolades. I do it to emotionally m
loves animals.

imal conservation. Whenever I text my Airbnb host
ith fleeting interest like "Wow that's a lot" and "I'm
' But her indifference is a small price to pay for the
d their short lives disoriented in a pasture of grass
hero, but I do not share this convenient anecdote for
ate you into realizing that I am a good person who

PICKLE JUICE

This reminds me of the famed Nicki Minaj monologue about pickle juice.

She said,
"You have to be a beast . . . that's the only way they respect you. I came up under Wayne and Wayne has his way of doing things. When Wayne walks on set and says don't talk to me have my music ready get the fuck up out of my face and I'm going to blow this motherfucking smoke up all in your face all day, it's cool. But every time I . . . every time I put my foot down and stand up for myself it's like, "We've heard about Nicki Minaj . . . Nicki Minaj shut down a photo shoot . . . no one wants to work with Nicki Minaj [cackles!]. But I'm glad you heard. Now when I come to a photo shoot let it be of quality, you know why? Because I put quality in what I do. I spend time and I spend energy and I spend effort and I spend everything I have, every fiber of my being, to give people quality. So if I turn up to a photo shoot and you got a $50 clothes budget and some sliced pickles on a motherfuckin' board, you know what? No. I am gonna leave. Is that wrong? Wanting more for myself? Wanting people to treat me with respect? You know what? Next time, they know better. But had I accepted the pickle juice, I would be drinking pickle juice right now. When I am assertive, I'm a bitch. When a man is assertive . . . he bossed up."

Nicki Minaj delivers this monologue in what looks like a poorly lit Mariott convention center, in a cotton-candy pink wig so big it has its own gravitational pull, as her then-boyfriend, Safaree of Love and Hip Hop fame, nods along and repeats what she says for emphasis. It's a lot to take in. But at the root of Nicki Minaj's Pickle Juice monologue, which I would put in the same Western canon as Shakespeare's Hamlet and Arthur Miller's Death of a Salesman, is a desire to be respected and revered as a female entrepreneur. She begins this diatribe referencing Lil Wayne. Godfather of the Young Money Cash Money Records empire that gave us hitmakers like Drake, Nicki Minaj, and Paris Hilton (who signed to that label in 2017). Lil Wayne, the great artist, and one of the best rappers in American history, who wrote the brilliant line "Safe sex is great sex you better wear a latex cuz you don't want a late text, an 'I think I'm late' text." Which is not only useful advice but also a brilliant use of internal rhyme. He also has the real genius line "Real Gs move in silence like lasagna." Which speaks for itself! But Nicki Minaj claims to have watched the child star (Wayne began rapping professionally at twelve years old) turned rock star (rebirth album!) be a total asshole to people and be sort of worshipped as a legend. Whereas Nicki Minaj feels that when she demands the same quality she is seen as a bitch. But she would rather be a bitch than have to drink pickle juice.

Instead, there should be questions that actually test prospective owners' knowledge, like: How many times have you watched that YouTube video about boundary training? And did you know that the Chow Chow is one of the oldest breeds in world history, belonging to Martha Stewart, Queen Victoria, and the Chinese emperors of yore, and while Chow Chows have beautiful coats, they also have more irritable temperaments and need experienced owners to work through their territorial behavior with other dogs? To which, of course, my answers would be *thirteen times* and *yes!*

I will continue on this journey to *Adopt Don't Shop*™, but the facts remain that so far the results have been ruff.[111]

---

111   See what I did there? A   n. Ruff . . . like "rough." See? I am mature enough to be
an owner! Give me a dog!!!

cornelia street

I rent a place on Cornelia Street, two doors down from the famed rental Taylor Swift muses about on *Lover*'s aptly titled song "Cornelia Street." I had not heard the song until I moved in and encountered several dozen tourists screaming the refrain outside my window every day.

I'd never walk Cornelia Street again.

I'd never walk Cornelia Street again.

For them, the West Village location is a mecca for their favorite pop song about the pain and power of nostalgia. For me, it is the first apartment I ever moved into alone.

I know exactly what held me back from this adulthood benchmark— fear. As a single young woman, I was afraid of the responsibility of being alone. I did not want to come back home after a long day and spend time alone. I did not want to shoulder the cost of my utility bills alone. But most importantly, I did not want to die alone— at the hands of an assailant who finds out that I, a single young woman, am all alone.

So, I got a dog.

Celine Dion is a black Chow Chow and everything I could have ever asked for if what I asked for was a guard dog that did not enjoy the company of people and was too cute to intimidate strangers. I named him after the Queen of Power Ballads because, much like the Canadian pop star, he is a diva.[112] At least once a day, I google "Does my dog like me?" because whenever I approach him to cuddle he runs away. My friends assure me that he likes me because he always wags his tail *before* running away from me.

I got Celine Dion to protect me, but my dog actively gets me into danger or passively watches me in danger. He is adorable and unfortunately he does not have a scary bone in his body.

One day, while we were walking on Cornelia Street, Celine Dion's prey drive kicked in and he tried to eat a baby bird. I dragged him away before he could attack the innocent fledgling, but it was too late. Not for the chick, but for me—the mother bird's maternal instincts also kicked in. She attacked my head, pecking at my scalp like I was in a black reboot of Hitchcock's *The Birds*. This scene took place in front of a very crowded outdoor restaurant. All of the patrons watched me run and scream in terror as my darling dog smiled, enjoying the "game" we were "playing" where the cost of *his* atonement was clumps of *my* hair.

Today, Celine Dion woke me up at 6:00 A.M. barking even though he's not a vocal dog. When trying to align the perfect breed for my

---

112   Also, he does not subscribe to gender, despite my veterinarian's insistence.

lifestyle, I found that Chow Chows love independence and hate to make noise . . . which is perfect, because I hate sounds and I love that Destiny's Child song. Sometimes my dog is so quiet, I forget I have a roommate who doesn't pay rent and eats all my food. Usually, when he wakes up early, I just wait for him to get bored and stop. But this time, he didn't stop. So to prevent a digestive episode on my immaculate rug, I decided to take him for a morning stroll through Washington Square Park.

I don't hate Washington Square Park. If anything, I am attracted to its chaotic energy. On any given day, there is a grown man blowing bubbles, a feeble lady feeding a hundred pigeons Panera bread, a gang of pizza rats enjoying dirty calzones, local chess lords who would've been grand masters were it not for the systemic inequality of opportunity, NYU students posing in caps and gowns irrespective of the time or day of the year, and posh one-percenters power-walking to their brownstones. I have traversed this park for years, first as an intern living in NYU housing at Rubin Hall, and now as an adult—I know exactly where and when to walk and not walk.

Washington Square Park after midnight is the worst. The park becomes home to stabbings, muggings, guys selling bad molly to NYU students, and a police state that doesn't deter any of the three. However, Washington Square Park at dusk? It is a close second in treachery. Now, please forgive me because I do not know what the culturally sensitive term for "crackhead" is. But one time, I walked through the northwest corner, where all the crack-dependent people[113] hung out, and learned that they thought my dog was sexy and wanted to pet him. I explained to this passionate[114] group that my dog hates people (including me) and bites.[115] One man replied, "Don't worry, I bite back," and then proceeded to chomp his missing teeth in the direction of my dog and me until we ran away. This would have been a perfect time for my ancient guard dog to protect me from the randomized threats of New York City parks. Instead, *I,* a young, single black woman, was his defender.

I understand the levels of chaotic evil that Washington Square Park commands; you have to get up pretty early in the morning to surprise me. That time was around 6:45 this morning. As I'm walking my dog, a man stands unusually close to me. He mutters something to me, which I can't decipher because I'm listening to an episode of the *New York Times*'s *The Daily* about how the Supreme Court is probably going to repeal affirmative action. He catches me off guard because he is so old, he looks like the ghost of James Madison. I don't know if Pop Pop wants directions or a hard candy, so I respond, "What?"

"That's right, you heard me."

No, I literally didn't hear you, I think.

I just keep walking.

---

113   This is said with no moral judgment. Addiction is a disease. Being a crack-dependent person does not make you a bad person; it just makes you a crackhead.

114   Read: hopped-up on stimulant drugs.

115   This is a lie. I have never seen my dog bite anything but beef jerky.

"You're—you're the strange one, not me! Go! You need to leave!"

Oh my gosh. I am so confused. Why is this frail old man yelling at me when he should be saving what little energy he has left to keep blocking the grim reaper's calls? Meanwhile, my very large dog looks up at him. Celine Dion trots on his distinctive stiff legs, wagging his bushy tail with his cute black tongue out, blissfully unaware that he is failing at his job as bodyguard.

I've been heckled by many racists, enough times to know I think he was trying to tell me to go back to where I came from but lacked an extensive dog-whistle vocabulary. The last time someone in New York City had told me to go back to where I came from, I was on the D train[116] with an ex-boyfriend. An elderly woman who looked like if Mrs. Claus practiced dark magic started mumbling to me in a Slavic language. At first, I thought she was an unwell person talking to herself, because she smelled like urine and had a shopping cart full of plastic bags. It wasn't until she kept repeating in broken English, "Fuck you, go back to Africa," and then did a sexually suggestive hand gesture that I realized that that old lady was a racist hater directing her ire at little ole me. I tapped my then boyfriend on the shoulder to inform him of the crone casting a racist spell on me, and he had the audacity to ask if I was sure I was hearing what I was hearing.

Once again, she repeated, "Fuck you, go back to Africa."

"Yes, I'm sure."

---

116   First mistake!

"How do you know that's directed to you?" I looked around the train. The only other black people stared at me as Confederate Claus got off at her stop.

I turned to them. "Did you hear that?"

"Yeah, that was crazy."

If there is one thing that black people are good at, it is immediately recognizing public displays of racism and then connecting over how brazen it was. Even though the subway car was full, my new black friends and I were the only ones who acknowledged Santa's Little Bigot. They confirmed what I saw and heard in plain daylight.

My ex and I broke up shortly after that.

But back to the present trauma: I run away from Robert E. Lee's grandpa and I see this black woman who's wearing a parks and recreation uniform. I try to get her attention.

"Yo . . . yo . . . yo . . ."

She ignores me . . . because it's 7:00 A.M., she's doing her job, and she doesn't want to talk to me. I respect this.

I badger, "Yo . . . yo . . . yo . . ."

She takes off her headphones that were definitely not playing music.

"Yo, be careful of that guy, like he's weird."

I point to him, and he looks back at us with venom in his eyes.

"He's wild. Be careful."

He nods. "Yeah, I said it."

I look at her. She looks back at me and then the two of us walk in the opposite direction of the creepy man. I go back to my apartment and I tell a different boyfriend about the incident. His first question is "How do you know he was racist?"

My brain begins to atrophy with nostalgia.

This conversation feels like déjà vu. Once again, I find myself in a position where I have to explain over and over again what I know to be true. People generally don't scream "I'm racist" as they commit hate crimes, even though a warning like that would be greatly appreciated.

Toni Morrison said that racism is a distraction. It keeps you explaining, over and over again, your reason for being, wasting your time proving to others what you know to be true. Once again, I find myself in the uncanny valley of the unplaceable, unshakeable fear that plagues me when I'm alone. I was walking my dog through Washington Square Park in the morning. It took so much effort to get to a point in my life where I rented a place on Cornelia Street on my own, and here I am having to justify my right to enjoy the same park as some random old white man. Somehow, I found myself accountable to another man I had never met. And then again, accountable for an explanation of why I was so afraid when he was the aggressor. I do not know how to communicate my intuition. But the caveat is that in this environment, if I do not waste my time on an explanation, like in my last relationship, this misunderstanding will leave me . . . alone.

So I explain in painstaking detail how I felt the way I did and why. In this conversation I find myself in a position I hate but am all too familiar with—caretaker. Just as I made sure to protect Celine Dion from the dangers that threatened me. I take care to rationalize the pathologies that inspired my anxiety disorder. In this connection, I help others help me not feel so alone. As I express love to feel love, I can't help question—who will be my caretaker?

I email my accountant:

> SUBJECT LINE: are guard dogs tax deductible
>
> hi
>
> hope you had a restful week!
>
> i want to buy a guard dog because I experienced what some would describe as a racial incident while with my dog—which makes me realize that my dog who i love is too cute to intimidate or protect me. if i wanted to get a trained guard dog, could i deduct it as a work expense?
>
> thanks for the help!

She responds promptly: No.

And I vow to never walk Washington Square Park again.

affirmative actions

Fran Lebowitz: *You know, there is this idea that all white people, especially men, achieve everything on their own and truthfully almost no one does. Most people need a little help.*

Ziwe: *Whenever I am like applying for a job, I imagine what a white guy would do.*

Fran Lebowitz: *What they do is get born.*

Ziwe: *And then, presidency! You talk about this in your* Vanity Fair *interview. It is not black geniuses you want to see exalted, it is the black imbeciles. That is when we will see true parity. And so I personally cannot wait 'til Ziwe Jr. is getting nepotism. Left and right, getting jobs she doesn't deserve. That is success.*

Fran Lebowitz: *Right, that is what I am saying. The Civil Rights Movement itself really worked for [what] they used to call the Talented Tenth, you know, but the Untalented Ninetieth—I did not say imbeciles, I just said untalented. The Untalented Ninetieth and its white counterpart, what about these people? Which is most people.*

Ziwe: *Shoutout to all the stupids, they deserve rights too. Stupid rights!*[117]

---

117   Excerpt from interview in *ZIWE* S1 E1, "55%," May 9, 2021, on Showtime.

PART 1

Every week, the entire student body of the New England prepara-
tory school I attended met in the chapel. Often, these meetings featured illustrious guest speakers who ranged from concert cellists
to former heads of state. Most guest speakers were unremarkable
to me. This was no fault of their own; I was a teenager. I didn't
appreciate the wisdom of accomplished adults. The only excep-
tion was, by far, the most disruptive speaker: Spike Lee.

Now, before I share this story, I'd like to state a couple of
disclaimers:

1.   Spike Lee is an icon, an absolute master of his craft as a
     director, writer, and producer.

2.   Spike Lee has fundamentally shaped racial discourse
     in America (and around the globe) and we all owe him a
     great debt.

3.   Spike Lee seems like a lovely man.

However, if I could, I would sue him for emotional damages. The
brilliant Spike Lee, who deserves to be celebrated for his contributions to cinema, ruined my and, conservatively speaking, every one
of my black peers' academic year, when one MLK Day he shared
radical opinions with students who were just hoping to feel good
about the "I Have a Dream" speech. A year after Dr. Ben Carson

had inspired a generation of future consultants to go make money[118] and buy things, Lee spoke about his Hurricane Katrina documentary, *When the Levees Broke*.

These are some of Spike Lee's direct quotes, documented in an archival student newspaper.[119]

On whether we're in a post-racial America . . .

400 years of slavery have not been wiped out by [President Barack] Obama's election.

On how he felt about speaking to a predominantly white student body of a school where the tuition was high . . .

I am happy I am here.

---

118   In many ways, Dr. Ben Carson was the perfect guest for Martin Luther King Day. Long before he was appointed secretary of housing and urban development, long before he was accused of falling asleep during a televised presidential debate, long before he claimed that Joseph (of Technicolor Dreamcoat fame) used pyramids for grain storage despite scientific evidence to the contrary, Ben Carson was a renowned neurosurgeon. One of Dr. Carson's most famous surgeries involved the complex procedure of separating Bangladeshi conjoined twins, Krishna and Trishna, who were connected at the head, allowing them to lead separate lives. He was a man of God and he had Gifted Hands™.

I will never forget Dr. Carson's speech, because he did not instill what the mainstream media would describe as an "age-appropriate" "uplifting message" for "children." At the end of Carson's address about his achievements and the fact that Cuba Gooding Jr. once played him in a biopic, Ben Carson began to wax poetically about his life. He said, "And if one day I lose my car and my house and everything I own, I will not have to worry."

Mr. Gifted Hands™ then paused for dramatic effect, presumably before he delivered a heartfelt message about the undying importance of family to the next generation of the best and the brightest leaders. But Ben Carson did not say that . . . To everyone's surprise, he continued, "I would buy it all back because I can afford to."

Wow. Ben Carson had escaped the clutches of inner-city Detroit to eventually receive the Presidential Medal of Freedom, the highest civilian honor in America. Yet, this was the defining message that he shared . . .? On Martin Luther King Day, no less! There was one lesson that I extrapolated here: Money. Is. Good.

119   Shoutout to student reporting! Democracy dies in the dark!

But the real bomb Spike Lee dropped was when [REDACTED] asked for his opinions on college admissions and Lee staunchly supported affirmative action, insisting that "race is a merit." This is not inherently a controversial statement, except that Lee made this assertion to a roomful of non-black competitive overachievers.[120]

The exchange went something like this:

> Spike Lee: Race is a social construct created to oppress. There is no such thing as white or black but merely those with power and those without. Without black Americans there is no culture. Affirmative action is to color correct the rigged scale. Race is a merit.
>
> *[hundreds of internal screams fill the century-old chapel]*
>
> [REDACTED STUDENT]: [imagine someone who was very passionate about model UN] Mr. Spike Lee, you say that race is a merit, but my question is that I think that success and accolades should go to those that work hard regardless of their race or gender. My question is that people should pull themselves up by their bootstraps to succeed and only then can they achieve the American Dream. My question is we are doing minorities, African Americans, Black Americans, no favors when we give them our spots on elite schools like Yale and Harvard . . .

---

120   No offense to this community, as I am a black competitive overachiever. I went to some of the best schools in the world, which I will not be naming because I want to send Ziwe Jr. there. This is all to say I had a wonderful time and they were a utopian haven of parity . . . pander pander pander [mic cuts out!]

Spike Lee: . . . I am waiting for a question.

For decades, I have tried and failed to repress this memory. Needless to say, this exchange between a world-renowned director and a high school senior did not go well. However, I do not blame Lee for being the core memory that fundamentally changed my brain chemistry. As a guest speaker on Martin Luther King Day, he had no idea[121] that saying "race was a merit" would detonate a bomb, leaving the black and brown population of the private school to catch stray shrapnel.

In true Spike Lee fashion, his opinions ~~ushered in a reign of terror~~ invited discourse! Unfortunately, this conversation happened to focus on affirmative action during the year I applied to college and got into [REDACTED] University, which a classmate remarked was "only because I was black." I wish I could say I had a funny retort in defense of myself, but I did not. I just stood there quietly. Six hours later, I thought of the perfect response while arguing with myself in the shower. But the conversation had moved on, so I would never have any use for it. At least, I thought I would not.

PART 2

I started my first year of [REDACTED] University without any doubt about the woman I thought I was. I was going to major in

---

121 Remember, this was before the Tumblr epoch. Teenagers did not use words like "intersectionality" and "BIPOC" and "microaggression" in everyday conversation. The first black president in American history had just gotten the job two years prior. Culturally, we were still figuring things out.

math and then spend my summers interning at Goldman Sachs and then have a beautiful life of excess surrounded by my harem of himbos because Ben Carson told me to. This dream, like most of my fantasies, came crashing down when I had to interact with humans. In math, we'd have to do these stupid group projects where we worked as a team. Everyone knows that teamwork makes the dream work!™ Collaboration is the foundation of success!™ However, only idiots and lazy people love group projects. They are a byproduct of the stupid rights lobby to hold advanced students who did the homework back from reaching their true potential. As someone who spent a lifetime being validated for my intellect, I was now suffering from the realization that no one really cared. During this one group project about rudimentary math, I insisted that I had the correct answer in a group full of pasty nerds. They did not believe me and instead wasted their breath trying to convince me that I was wrong. When our time was up, I put my answer down and they put their answers down and I was right and they were . . . them. This was the day I decided I would no longer be majoring in math or pursuing a career in finance, as the thought of spending my life trying to convince a bunch of fuglies[122] to listen to me was not something I could commit to.

So, I pivoted. I majored in African American studies and I applied for a certificate in creative writing in poetry. I had a wonderful professor named Rachel Webster, who, as I never noticed until recently, shares her last name with the famous dictionary. I never confronted her about this coincidence, and it is one of my great-

---

122   Not every man in finance is fugly. That is an incredibly rude thing to say. Patrick Bateman is so hot and he has an incredible apartment. What a catch!

est regrets in life. Rachel Webster was an ethereal being, and my strongest memory of her is stumbling upon her smelling a cherry-blossom tree outside the university library, which resembled a maximum-security prison. I will never shake the image of watching her literally stop to smell the flowers, and to this day I frequently meander on my walks to sniff flora, not because I care about their scent but because I want onlookers to cherish a whimsical memory of me in the same way.

I only studied poetry because it was a discipline that required the least amount of reading. The margins were so big and the font was so large, it was easy to ingest a poem during class and bullshit about its meaning without betraying my lack of preparation. Yet Rachel Webster was a professor who believed in all her students and called me out when I complained about being bored. She once asked me if I had read every book and when I said no, she told me I had something to do.[123]

In addition to introducing me to great poets like D. A. Powell and Anne Carson and John Ashbery, Rachel Webster encouraged me to engage with race in my writing, which marked the first time I had explored this subject creatively. One time in class, a discussion on National Book Award winner Nikky Finney's *Head Off & Split* turned to a conversation about Hurricane Katrina, as conversations often do in liberal arts schools where everyone is speaking out of their depth. Some of my classmates insisted that the tragedy in New Orleans where thousands of poor, mostly black citizens were stranded for days without food, water, and electricity had nothing to do with race.

---

123   Okay, Rachel Webster, drag me . . .

I remember listening intently, knowing that three years prior, I had watched Spike Lee speak about his documentary *When the Levees Broke*. Lee's conversations around the film ushered in conversations about not only race in New Orleans, Louisiana, but race in American colleges.

This had been the exact moment he was talking about: My merit for attending a Big Ten university in part was to share my perspective in this discourse. After all, according to my old classmate, I had only gotten into this school because I was black. I wondered how many of my peers thought this about me.

I had watched the documentary and even spoken to the director about his work. But all I could muster was "You do not know what you're talking about." Of that I was certain. Now, why a twenty-one-year-old Midwest native could not connect that one of the deadliest natural disasters in American history that disproportionately affected black neighborhoods was "about race," I did not have the words to express.

Rachel Webster, who had watched in slow motion as discourse devolved from bad to worse, wrapped the conversation in the neatest bow she could.

"I do not understand how you can look at what happened in New Orleans and not think it is about race."

Rachel Webster then packed her stuff and floated out of the classroom, leaving us to revel in our folly. It was a defining moment in my academic career. She taught us not only that were we wrong, but also that we could not even see how narrow our perspectives were. Slowly, I learned how to put those feelings into words.

PART 3

Most of my poems corresponded to whatever I was learning that week in my African American studies classes. One week, we learned about black radicals. I had been particularly attracted to Malcolm X due to his symmetrical face and the unprompted insults he directed at his more pacifist contemporaries, because I famously love mess.

Here is the first poem I ever wrote about race in Rachel Webster's poetry class:

At the Intersection of Martin Luther King and Frederick
Douglass Boulevard
By: Ziwe

Lansing, Michigan

Hunched over the kitchen stove
Brittle Louise Little salted boiled grass
For her eight grey children.
Earl Little, a Garveyite,
Preached African prosperity—
Respect and redemption,
And his voice trembled the earth,
Like the scramble of a mob,
Until the men in cotton sheets

Left Earl's little entrails
Along the long dirt road.
Soon, the weight of eight
Grey children broke Brittle
Louise Little, delivering her
To Kalamazoo State Hospital,
And her children
to the state-certified
foster homes, that were shabby
And barren and overflowing
With other little black children
That were pushed from stranger to
Stranger, until they met
Adulthood and the state pushed
Them their hard, filthy cots
To the festering streets.

"Who taught you to hate
yourself from the top of your head
To the soles of your feet?"

Harlem, New York

We saw savage beasts, wallowing
With the roaches in dilapidated projects,
As school-aged prostitutes reclined on 155th and
Washington Heights,
Bestowing fresh treats to their chocolate Daddies,
And Welfare Queens rationed stale bread and rotting
peaches
For their children and cousins and nephews and nieces,

Homeless men rode the M1 from Harlem to East Village
And then East Village to Harlem, defrosting as they
drank
Malt liquor from the government's calloused bosom,
This was the promised land.

By age fifteen, sweet brother Malcolm,
Relished in the mud like swine,
Lying, cheating, stealing, drug dealing,
Pimping, drinking, gambling, prostituting
until he fell into a concrete cell, adorned
With black iron windows and doors,
He asked himself,

"Who taught you to hate
yourself from the top of your head
To the soles of your feet?"

We saw deformed brutes,
So we bleached our skin,
Burning melanin like coal,
Littering our dried ashes
along the trash infested streets.
We silenced our feral tendrils,
Saturating them in acid,
Our Kinky hair now
smooth like cotton.
We plucked our robust noses
Each morning, dark blood
Crusting under our
Chipped fingernails,

until they were
pointed and proper,
Like the Americans
That drove thunderbirds,
And wore dungarees,
And smiled on TV.
Like the Americans that
Disfigured a whistling Chicago boy
In the swamps of Mississippi,
Like the Americans that burned
Schoolgirls alive in the
16th Street Baptist Church
On a Sunday morning.
Like Americans that
Promised forty acres and a mule
But gave inferior housing and
Niggardly wages.

Sweet brother Malcolm X,
Reformed liar, cheater, thief, drug dealer,
Pimp, drunk, gambler, prostitute
Placed a vanity mirror
At the corner of Martin Luther King
and Frederick Douglass Boulevard,
And asked

"Who taught you to hate
yourself from the top of your head
To the soles of your feet?"

Malcolm saw beauty.

> He saw Africans kidnapped
> From a promised land,
> Dragged across the Atlantic by a jagged noose
> Attached to a lemon tree.
> He saw kings and queens,
> With skin like gold,
> Black coils dense as the congo rainforest,
> Noses flat as the horizon.
> And soon we began to see the same.

Poetry is cringe. At twenty-one years old, I took myself too seriously as an artist. I believed that my words could end world hunger, bring about world peace, and dismantle global apartheid at the same time. I don't think I ever had fun writing a poem, but I had a lot of fun rereading them and thinking, *Wow, I freaked it.* Like Dorothy Parker, I hated writing but I loved having written. Between that starting point and the end product was a black hole of tedious, endless work. But that's how I found my inner voice. Not the one that I had affected to maneuver through private institutions or the one that I thought would be a great inner voice to have based on market research of other people's inner voices. This was the one that was with me all along. When friends talk about doing ayahuasca, they note the purging cleanse of nausea paired with profound hallucinations in which they play a game of pickup basketball with Jesus and their great-aunt Thelma. On the other side of their weird psychedelic pilgrimage, they experience ego death—feeling one with themselves and the universe, as if everything they needed was always right in front of them.

Ego death in writing is not that glamorous. Imagine pushing a boulder up a steep hill with your bare hands. It's tiring, difficult, monotonous. But through these series of affirmative actions, at the very least you believe that you'll reach the top, even if it's more likely that the boulder rolls back down and you must start again. Contrary to Carrie Bradshaw propaganda, this is the glamour of writing. It is never-ending work. For me, peace comes from granting myself the grace of being bad. *Everything is badly illuminated. Extremely bad and incredibly bad close-up.* My work was often so inconsistent in its voice and tone and point that it was impressive. But in that abyss where the only matter that exists is the faint promise of my potential, I wallowed in the volume of my bad words, tinkering away.

Here is the last poem I wrote in college:

(Black) Poet
By: ziwe
No great poet has ever been afraid
Of being himself. And I doubted then,
That with his desire to run away
Spiritually from his race, this boy
Would ever be a great poet.

–Langston Hughes
"The Negro Artist and the Racial Mountain"

A peacock crosses my course,
Emerald plumes bloom
As his slack hem anoints
The grove he roams.

His coat, a sapphire blue,

Captures the sun's gloss.
His pupils, black as god's earth,
Reflect my nude

Dress—the neutral contrasts
My dark flesh, accentuating
The salt and sweat
That bloat my skin.

In his beauty, I begin to
Question if my identity
is from without or within,
if below this layer

my blood runs black
And thick, or if
Like Langston's boy,
I itch to be a privileged poet

That sits at the zoo
To discuss that all the
Animals are caged except
The peacocks and the humans,

Rather than the cleaning
women's knocked knees,
Stiff and pocked, from nights
Scrubbing feces off swines' pens.

I am not great.

I am a fallible beast with two lips and
Two breasts for symmetry,
two ears, one spine for balance,
And two eyes that see the clouds

And earth never converge.
Stunted by the cast of my form,
I am the black poet
Bound by duty to women

That wade through sewage,
Clutching infants against slack bosoms.
Flicking dried tongues against
Cracked lips as they plead to
Deaf gods—presidents, uplink vans,
And helicopters, that the sharp
Odor of corpses drifting
Up Common Street to the
Superdome, will not stir
Their angels from their shallow
Slumber.

Duty is a loaded gun
Pressed against my temple,
And it sights me into
the world of monochrome

Where the poetry is live
Like blues crooners and
Catwalks and beat breakers
and spades players and

Teeth and lemon trees and
Drug raids and red riots
That lit baltimore, chicago,
los angeles, new york, oakland,
philadelphia, washington
Ablaze, hemorrhaging the page
Creating Baraka's Black Art.

Must I sing this cry?

The peacock crows in technicolor,
As gaunt lions sip
from ponds, pliant giraffes
pluck leaves from pygmy trees,

And shrewd turtles grey beneath
the heat-lamp's gaze,
Undeterred by the guttural screech
Because all understand his call.

I shadow him to a clouded fountain,
Cherubs mist water along the
Marble edges as children resign
Silver dollars and wishes to gods.

His feathers extend
beyond east and west
and one hundred eyes
Peer through my soul.

There is a dramatic difference between my first and last poem. Ira Glass once spoke on the early stages of creativity:

> For the first couple years you make stuff, it's just not that good. It's trying to be good, it has potential, but it's not. But your taste, the thing that got you into the game, is still killer. And your taste is why your work disappoints you. . . . We all go through this. . . . It is only by going through a volume of work that you will close that gap, and your work will be as good as your ambitions.

Whenever my hyper-fixation on making things that were "quality" gave me writer's block, I would turn to the quantity game of just creating until I found the exact words that I didn't know I was missing. I stopped trying to force my voice and submitted to the chords that always struck with repetition. So, if there are any young artists reading this book, my best advice is that you should never be afraid of being bad. Embrace the cringe. The only way to get good is by spending countless hours working on your craft. It took me too long to understand why I felt compelled to write, but eventually I realized that my life experiences had offered me the merit of something unique to say. I was determined to share my newfound voice, but how? I loved poetry, but unless you are the poet laureate or have a sizable trust fund, there is very little money to eat anything other than potatoes and loose-leaf paper. I owed it to my parents, who sacrificed so much to immigrate to America, to not become a starving artist. I am more than a stereotype.[124]

---

124   This is not a knock on the profession of poetry but rather a critique of our country's lack of social safety nets for artists. We have a caste system where the only people who can afford to

Despite a degree from [REDACTED], I felt financially insecure about my career pursuits.

PART 4

It was perfect timing when my college roommate forwarded info on an internship.

Comedy Central's Summer School Program!

Tuesday, October 30, 2–4pm

This internship program targets young comedy writers of color to receive hands-on experience in a variety of departments, make invaluable industry contacts, and hone their writing skills while working side-by-side with some of the best in the comedy business, including the award-winning staffs of "The Colbert Report" and "The Daily Show with Jon Stewart."

A diversity program. Once again Spike Lee's beloved affirmative action had reared its head into my Negro business. It was the racial mountain that I could not avoid.

Six years prior, I had attended my first diversity program, called PALS, where underprivileged advanced students were bused to

---

create art for a living come from generations of wealth. If the arts continue to be affordable only for those with means, we are going to have a country full of poets who write about teakwood, Bain Capital, and apéritifs that pair well with champagne.

TEAM PLAYING

I once worked at a job that had a mandatory book club that offered readings about how employees could self-actualize as humans. Most of the books were unsubtle propaganda that circled around three points: Do not unionize under any circumstances because that would break the unspoken trust between you and the corporation that pays you minimum wage with no benefits. Remember that the company is your family, and everyone has a distinct role in this family; for example, you are the dog. Going to the bathroom on company time is wage theft.

No disrespect to corporate America, but if an employer says that your workplace is a family, you are about to witness some of the most heinous labor rights violations in world history. Avoid these places like the plague, because they will eventually pay someone $250/hr to fire all the $15/hr employees because they are "too expensive." I was twenty-one years old when I learned that consulting was a real job that paid real money. Prior to my senior year of college, I just assumed that professional consultants were a wives' tale like Bigfoot or the Loch Ness Monster. I had never met a consultant before. But suddenly, my junior winter, half of my class was doing logic tests (?) and word puzzles (?) in the hopes that they would be offered a premier internship position at a top-tier firm—McKinsey, Bain & Company, Deloitte, etc. If you

see one of these youthful business-casual employees sniffing around, there are about to be mass layoffs.

Sometimes setting boundaries for yourself is a sign of success. Oprah says that "no" is a full sentence.

If you want clear communication, get it in writing.

"The meeting industrial complex" is a term I've coined to refer to the part of office jobs that I despise the most. In layman's terms, it is the economy of meetings. Think of it as your job's commitment to occupying as much of your time as humanly possible with needless face time on Zoom and in person. In my line of work, we meet for everything. We have meetings to discuss when the next meetings should be. We have meetings to discuss the meetings we just met about. We have meetings to say that the meetings have been set and we will see you at the next meeting. We have meetings to summarize the writing and then additional meetings to direct what the next bits of writing should say. There are so many meetings it's hard to find time to actually do the work you're meeting about. Are these meetings productive? Absolutely not. But if you miss the meeting, you alienate yourself from your team, coming across as uncommitted. While I enjoy speaking to people who share my professional interests, meetings are elaborate performances without the compensatory applause. For me, there is an extensive amount of research I need to do before I enter a meeting. The anticipation of these meetings takes up so much time that I have to clear at least three hours before and after the meeting to silently decompress the anxiety meetings fill me with. This eliminates any opportunity for creative work. One meeting will ruin my entire workday.

a neighboring high school in a wealthy town and tutored by students, half of whom genuinely wanted to help and the other half of whom were hoping to pad their résumés with extracurricular activities for college admissions. Created by literal saint and famed bird-watcher Tom Cone, the program exposed rising sixth- and seventh-graders to a new world. This included learning to play chess and tennis, traipsing through the school's four dining halls, and orienteering, the act of using compasses to navigate, during humid Massachusetts summers at high noon. It allowed young students to see a quality of education outside the underfunded public school system, prompting most participants to apply to local private schools to continue their pursuit of quality education. All of us applied to attend the school where that diversity program took place. I was the only one to get in. That affirmative action led me to my prestigious New England boarding school.

When Junot Díaz spoke at that same boarding school, he left a big impression. Some would say that the Pulitzer Prize–winning author did not do a great job. Díaz would not stop swearing during his speech. We knew that he was not supposed to swear because he repeatedly apologized by saying, "I am so sorry I'm swearing, they told me not to swear."

Later in the day, he hosted a breakout session for aspiring writers from my fancy prep school and visiting students from Lawrence, the "underprivileged" neighboring city that was famous throughout Essex County for its "abject" poverty.[125] In the Community and Multicultural Development office, the two groups of students waited for Díaz in silence despite the fact that we all had more in common than a shared border between the two towns. The only thing that could break the tension was Díaz himself, who I should note was about forty-five minutes late.[126] He started the exclusive conversation by lambasting the merits of the very private institution that was paying for him to speak. He said something along the lines of "This private high school shouldn't exist, and I am here giving advice[127] to these privileged kids when I should be talking to *you*." He then stared directly at the brown kids bused from the neighboring city. I remember a bunch of my classmates thinking he was an asshole, but I thought he was so funny. Maybe because that sort of directness was rare in those spaces. Or maybe because that "inner-city ghetto" that had always been the punch line to jokes about poverty was the city I was born and raised in.

While I felt pride about the exclusive opportunity of abandoning overcrowded classrooms and unchallenging curriculum, I always felt deep shame about how I did it and where I was from. Lawrence was a punch line, and it was affirmative action that allowed

---

125   The immigrant city is actually more or less working class, with some industrial decline, but nuance is lost on stereotypes.

126   I believe he was traveling from an adjacent building.

127   He also said that it was okay to turn in your manuscript whenever it was ready, advice I have internalized, much to my editors' chagrin. It took him ten years to write *The Brief Wondrous Life of Oscar Wao*, a novel that chronicled a Dominican coming-of-age story both past and present. It resonated with me as someone from Lawrence, Massachusetts, a city full of Dominicans, and it is the reason this book has footnotes.

me to enter the boarding school without any political connections or money for the $51,000-a-year tuition. Never mind that I had an immaculate report card of straight As and I was so committed to the business of school that I had perfect attendance from kindergarten to eighth grade.[128] I had every right to be there. Still, I could not shake the feeling that I was an imposter.

Nearly eight years later, I was staring down the barrel of the same fate. I could apply to the internship that offered ten people of color the opportunity to get their foot in the door of the entertainment industry, or I could listen to my peers who admonished the program as unfair. But life was unfair. Prior to this, my life at college consisted of me applying to club after club to no avail. I was rejected from the improv troupe Mee-Ow, and I was rejected from the other improv troupe, Out Da Box.[129] But I did not let this rejection stop me from putting myself out there. Chris Rock founded the internship program, nicknamed Rockterns as in Chris Rock Interns, because he thought people of color were underrepresented in the creative behind-the-scenes roles. I heard that Donald Glover had done it a couple of years prior, and I wanted to have a career like his. So, I applied. And I got in—suddenly I was a Rocktern.

There are many jokes to be made about diversity programs and the ways in which corporations champion them as a badge of progress rather than delayed justice. These force a sort of integration in which young, vulnerable people of color are ushered into institutions and forced to either sink or swim. It is not an easy feat, nei-

---

128   You read that correctly. #NoDaysOff

129   Do you know the psychological toll it takes on a human being to be rejected from two (2) improv troupes? My spirit was broken like a [IMPROVISE A PUNCH LINE YOURSELF]!

ther on the underappreciated job of the creative who wedges the door open behind them nor on the aspiring creatives who learn the hard way that you really have to work twice as hard. However, these programs do make great recruitment tools when they enlist the smiling black friends to cover newsletters and college magazines. These programs are integral to corporate America but also reflect W. E. B Du Bois's Talented Tenth mentality.

And now for some historical context!

In 1903, educator and author W. E. B Du Bois published an essay explaining that racial advancement for black people rested on the brilliant 10 percent of the community receiving a classical education so that they could go back to their communities and properly lead. This was in direct contrast to Booker T. Washington's "Atlanta Compromise," which expressed that black people should focus on vocational training so that they had the labor skills needed to get industrial jobs.

As it stands, programs that I have participated in like PALS and Rockterns have undoubtedly propelled me to a level of success. This is not to take away from my efforts. If you knew how hard I worked you'd be embarrassed for me. But who would have thought someone with two prestigious private school degrees would go on to achieve professional success? Well . . . everyone would think that. My path is surprising only if you lack a fundamental understanding of how black people who do not play basketball or sing like a siren break through into power structures. It takes exceptional palatability, acute cunning undercut only by extreme social intelligence, to break the racial barriers of being the first black editor at the *Harvard Law Review* and then eventually the first black president. Black friends who attend private institutions are not better or smarter. They are lucky. They are lucky that they were not born at a different time or in a different city or with different parents or any other slight sliding door adjustments to nature vs. nurture that would derail their life path. But it takes a certain mettle to be able to cut your teeth in a hostile environment and come out smiling.

But what about the other 90 percent of black people of average intellect and average athletic ability, looks, and vocal talent? The Untalented Ninetieth. At my most hopeful, my success could be a sign of parity. But at my most pessimistic, my arc reflects that the system works as designed. That a black woman conditioned through private school and entrenched in a structurally powerful network could thrive under those conditions points to a need for programs that not only open the door, but build their own house. Some individuals have pioneered these models, like Issa Rae, Jordan Peele, Quinta Brunson, Oprah Winfrey, Denzel Washington, and Tyler Perry—what he has done for the Atlanta film industry, which he single-handedly imagined into fruition, regardless of what one thinks about the quality of his wigs.

I am an outlier. My story is incredibly rare and, much like that of a mythical hero, starts with the literal death of a parent. I would not be here without generations of trauma. Yet to achieve racial advancement, there need to be ways other than the divine alignment of living a stone's throw away from one of the best private schools in the world and then attending a midwestern college by happenstance because I thought New England was getting boring. If my career is a living testament of anything, let it be that one opportunity is not enough. It is a series of cracked-open windows and doors that have gotten me into a position of what I would describe as fleeting power. We need as many opportunities as possible. To fail, to be bad, and then to eventually succeed. Even if it is as a regional manager at a Bonobos. The flexibility to fail comes in part with your health care not hanging in the ether after one false step at work. Things like universal basic income, health care, and housing, while good for all people, are really great for marginalized people. But more importantly, these opportunities are the first steps in addressing what we learned during the summer of 2020, which is that there is an undeniable benefit to being white in America, and to acknowledge that is not enough. The journey starts with using power to rectify the centuries-long imbalance.

No influence is too small or fleeting. Take the recommendation letter that my professor Rachel Webster wrote for my first internship. While I was writing this book, I asked her to send it.

Dear [REDACTED],

I am writing to enthusiastically recommend Ziwe Fumudoh for the internship with Comedy Central. I met Ziwe last year when she was in my class, English 206, Reading and Writing Poetry, and my Creative Writing colleagues and I selected her, along with just 13 other students, for our Advanced (yearlong) Sequence in Poetry. In this sequence, I have met with Ziwe and the other students twice a week since the beginning of fall term, and have gotten to know Ziwe well, both as a writer and as a student.

Ziwe is an uncommonly hard worker and original thinker, and she has had us all laughing hard at times in class. At other times, she has prodded us to think about poems and ideas more deeply and broadly. I have been especially impressed by her ability to hold her own point of view with grace, dignity and strength, in conversations with people who do not always understand or share her level of lived complexity. She seems to know well when to speak up and when to just listen and observe. Ziwe is very much of our own time and popular culture—she is connected to its wavelengths and even its absurdities—and yet she is able to offer the smart, unique perspective necessary to good comedy. I trust that Ziwe would make fun of herself when efficacious; would rise above situations to see them clearly; and would work hard—even indefatigably—to write and revise, learn and apprentice in a way exceeding expectations. I know that she would bring enthusiasm, talent, and high energy to the task, and I think that she would be an enlivening presence for those around her. She is fun to be with, and yet a profound, intense person. And she is quite a talented writer.

Thus, I recommend Ziwe [REDACTED] without reservations for this opportunity. I would be happy to answer any questions about this recommendation and can be reached at [REDACTED] or [REDACTED].

Thank you for your consideration and very best wishes,

Rachel Webster

Artist in Residence
Poetry

Rachel Webster used her voice, as a professor, as an artist, to help a young black woman get an opportunity to fail. She had no idea the ripple effect that this would have on my life or the lives of other young black women who appreciate my work and feel inspired to pave their own way. And while the unmitigated truth is that our institutions need sweeping reform, the arc of the universe is long, which means progress can be slow and uneven. But there are individuals in our lives who need our voice today. Politics are personal.

Were it not for these diversity programs, in which I participated alongside other noted industry titans like Sudi Green, Berhana, and Stefani Robinson, I would not have understood just how attainable entering the entertainment industry was. With my Nigerian upbringing, I had been raised to believe that there were only three professions: Doctor, Lawyer, and/or Wife. I had no concept of what a job in television or film could possibly look like or that to many it was just a day job with an office. Affirmative action changed that. It exposed me to the regular people who made these shows and networks run.

During the internship, every week a guest speaker would come to inspire us to achieve our American Dreams™. Sometimes it was someone in the marketing department talking about how marketing was their dream; other times it was someone in the development department talking about how finding the next *Workaholics* was their dream. One time, Aasif Mandvi, a correspondent on *The Daily Show*, spoke to us about how he broke into the industry. His advice was simple: Do not take no for an answer and do not wait for permission; go make opportunities for yourself no matter how embarrassing it may seem.

So, I did just that. I went and looked for every opportunity I could to pursue writing comedy. And I was rejected from them all.[130] I was rejected from the comedy newspaper. I was rejected from the stand-up club. I was rejected from the sketch comedy club, only to reapply in a year and get appointed to their marketing department.[131] When it comes to comedy, all I could do was fail. But I did not let being bad stop me.

I started a humor magazine. I built a large following on Twitter. And I got an internship that led to a job in New York as a writing assistant, which led to my first TV writing job, which led to another job and another job and eventually led to my own talk show on the same network. I wish I could say that my success was a straight path, but it did not feel that way when I was writing during hostess shifts at a barbecue restaurant in Union Square.

And all of this was possible because of Spike Lee's beloved affirmative action. Years later as my career blew up, the classmate who told me I only got into college because I was black slid into my direct messages on Instagram. He saw me on the cover of *New York* magazine next to Spike Lee.[132] He told me how proud he was of my success and how he always believed in me. He had forgotten our exchange eleven years prior even though I could never

---

130   I bet you thought this was going to be a happy ending? No. I was not happy.

131   They felt bad for me and admired my Twitter following so they entasked me with promoting the videos I was not technically welcomed to write or be in. I did not do a good job. One day the president pulled me aside at the student center to lecture me on how I needed to take my unpaid labor of marketing niche sketch comedy videos more seriously. I disassociated during the whole lecture and never posted about the group again . . . until now. Much like Michael Jordan, I was initially rejected only to come back with a vengeance and drop 38 points with a 103-degree fever. Let this be a lesson: No one knows what they are talking about, especially college students.

132   And Ice Spice!

shake that memory. I left the message unread for a week before I responded. That's the problem with grudges. I was holding on to a grievance he did not even know existed. In that moment no response would have brought me the satisfaction of knowing that *this* black friend had proved him wrong. I had spent hours arguing in the shower preparing my comeback, but he would not get the privilege of hearing the voice I found between adolescence and adulthood: *"Jealousy is a disease, bitch."*

BIPOC

Until very recently, I assumed that the acronym "BIPOC" meant "bisexual people of color." As in sexually fluid people of color. It stands for Black, Indigenous, People of Color. BIPOC is such an interesting catchall to describe the wide umbrella that covers every person on earth who is not white. Not only is that a lot of people, but it covers a diverse array of thought.

My cynicism toward the term is best explained with a metaphor from *Real Housewives of New Jersey*. Describing the feud between her husband, Joe, and his sister, Teresa Giudice, Melissa Gorga said, "Sadam Hussein is someone's brother but that doesn't mean he's a good person." There is no inherent value in the description of "brother," as there is no inherent value in the description of "people of color." Black Indigenous people of color are not a monolith: Some of us are valedictorians, and others never harbored weapons of mass destruction.

Sprinkling people of color at an event does not guarantee a virtuous[133] outcome. This is symbolic representation vs. actual representation. Did you know that everyone in al-Qaeda is a person of color? It is 99.99% BIPOC. That doesn't exactly mean that what they are doing is for diversity, equity, and inclusion. I don't know what they're doing because I was in public school when the US invaded Iraq. Regardless, I think we have to have more stringent definitions of what we want out of diversity.

That statement made me think.

---

133   In *Between the World and Me*, Ta-Nehisi Coates said, "There is nothing inherently virtuous in being oppressed, and there is no inherent vice in being privileged. Foot Locker does not hire you because you are black, and Harvard does not reject you because you are white. This is not the work of elites seeking to crush the poor; it is the work of an entire society, elites and non-elites alike."

my body of work

One of my first memories was my mother informing me that giving birth to me ruined her body. I didn't exactly understand the science behind how pregnancy and childbirth change a woman's physiology. I still don't. But I understood that my body is the reason my mother didn't like her body anymore. As a result, I developed a strange relationship with my own.

I'm writing this essay in JFK Airport. I just got through airport security, where the TSA agents put their hands between my legs. They claim it's because the metal detector flagged an obstruction, which is also the reason they pat down my braids, apparently. I'm not sure why it takes three people to feel me up, but I guess those are the conditions of a post–9/11 America. One agent asks me what I do for a living. I tell them I'm a writer.

I'm most self-conscious about my body when I travel. Sometimes a corporate sponsor offers me an airport greeter, which is the person who holds a little sign that says your name, takes your bags, and whizzes you through every line. Today, my New York greeter apologized to me for the commotion at arrivals. There were several sets of parents traveling with their screaming children. She

said she wished there was a separate terminal for *them*. Reading
between the lines, I am pretty sure she was advocating for segregation. I thought about telling her that I didn't pay for my flight.
That the reason she was my greeter was because I was good at
posting things on the internet. That that same internet was collecting all of our data and working very hard to replace us with
AI. That in fifteen years I didn't think either of us would have a
job. That we should buy property and start a commune before
it's too late because without universal health care, medicine, and
housing we'd probably be royally fucked. Instead I just stared at
her behind my mask and sunglasses. She dropped me off at an
airport lounge, which are usually nice, but this one was just a separate terminal for Air France customers. Now that I think of it,
it's class-segregated seating. Going through customs in Paris, a
man yelled at us for cutting him in line. I felt bad. The airport was
crowded. It was the day of a mass strike. The country had pushed
the retirement age back from sixty-two to sixty-five. As a result, the
airports, trains, and public transit were experiencing mass delays.
I learned all of this in a memo served with my hotel's room service.
I think we're not too far from a labor movement. Orcas have been
capsizing yachts all over the world. It's only a matter of time before
the rest of us join them. The French agent rolled his eyes. There
were more pressing issues. Then, he said that I had a dancer's
body. Horniness is embarrassing.

I know I have petite privilege. But this benefit compounded after
I was bedridden for one week, unable to consume anything but
content. In this case it was all thirteen parts of the documentary
The Staircase.[134] Thanks to the deadly virus that almost killed me,

---

134   You think an owl killed that woman? Don't be so naive!

I lost a considerable amount of weight. A fact about myself I wasn't aware of until I started fittings for my show. I didn't own a scale at the time, but as I was trying on sample sizes, my coworkers were mystified by the fact that everything fit perfectly. I could see in real time the financial advantages of fitting samples. This meant it was easier to source, which saved my costume team money and time. Suddenly, I was very aware that my body was not just for the function of my day-to-day life but for the function of my work.

There is an inherent conflict in losing weight as a result of illness and being lauded for it. But how could I complain? Yes, I was hovering at a weight I had not been at since high school. Yes, I was eating unseasoned Westville salmon and spinach every day for nine months. Yes, I was always freezing. However, I was doing this for work. That's the cost of doing business. This is my job as a laborer.

I remember watching the E! News pre-show as a kid and listening to dozens of Polly Pocket–size starlets talk about how they got camera-ready for the big awards shows. Some mentioned facials, others discussed their glam routine, but almost all referred to the labor of losing weight to fit in "the dress." Whether that was immersing their body in an infrared sauna to sweat out excess fat; or committing to a carb-free, fat-free, taste bud–free diet; or working out with an exclusive trainer to get their ass, abs, and arms tight, women were pressured to share their "secret" to the perfect (read: thin) body. I associated the determination these women displayed and the cavalier intrusions the correspondents lobbed as a fact of womanhood. Back then, it was SlimFast or Weight Watchers; now it's Ozempic. I think it's easy to blame the women who perpetuate this insidious diet culture. Only really, I stopped to wonder if the problem was that our bodies belonged to our benefactors.

Society likes to discard women who have lost their sexual appeal due to the natural process of aging. That's why I identify as nineteen. Goo goo gah gah. It's old enough to be legal while still young enough to be a sexual object. Logic serves that if I never age, I can't be thrown away.

It's not that I am inherently afraid of aging. There are elements to it I find confusing, like the fact that it gets harder and harder to sit on the floor; whereas I spent my childhood sitting crisscross applesauce for hours on end. But aging is exciting to me. I long to be a powerful working woman in my forties who does not care what people think about me or my polka-dot Bentley. But the unavoidable question for an aging woman is children.

The jury is still out on whether or not I want kids. Despite Evangelicals' best efforts, as of June 2023 in New York City, it's still my body and choice. On the one hand, I believe in global warming and I haven't made enough money to ensure my future progeny can afford a home next to Jeff Bezos on the Mars colony. On the other hand, I have amazing genes that deserve to be preserved for humanity's sake. As of publication, this is still my real[135] face! Whereas men can have children until their semen turns to dust,

---

135   People like to think there is an award for not getting plastic surgery, but there is nothing other than the money and time you save not being under the knife. I don't know where I stand on the politics of plastic surgery. If something bothers you and you have the opportunity, why not fix it? But where does empowering body modifications end and body dysmorphia begin? I love when people are forthcoming about the work they have had done, as it demystifies the unrealistic beauty standard.

However, is the public entitled to know every modification you've made to your body? I don't know. At a reunion, Andy Cohen once asked *Real Housewives of Beverly Hills* star Dorit Kemsley, "Dorit, Judy from Fort Smith, Arkansas, wants to know how your gigantic breast implants affect your mammograms?" This is one of the most influential questions of my career, as I find this question to be so rude, invasive, and inappropriate. This is a professional boundary I would never cross. While I am interested in the answer, I do not feel comfortable confronting women about their bodies because it is so personal. I posited that if Andy could ask this question to

after thirty-five years, pregnant women are classified as geriatric.

I was okay with my indecision until I read an article about a woman's body. It was the December profile on Jennifer Aniston in *Allure* where she told writer Danielle Pergament, "I would've given anything if someone had said to me, 'Freeze your eggs. Do yourself a favor.' You just don't think it. So here I am today. The ship has sailed."

My first thought was, if Rachel Greene from *Friends* says I should freeze my eggs, I guess I have to freeze my eggs.

So I went to a treatment center. I listened closely as the doctor informed me about the process.

> *You have to inject yourself with hormone shots every day. You can't travel a month before egg retrieval because your ovaries can twist and you can DIE. You have to pay rent for the eggs every year until you use them or terminate them. The younger you are when you retrieve your eggs, the more likely the eggs are to not be rotten. Egg retrieval is short and painless because you're under anesthesia; the real discomfort comes from the bloating that hormones prompt. It costs like $20,000 and there is no guarantee that it'll work.*

It was so expensive. My union health insurance covered part of the process but not enough. It reminded me that one-third of all

---

a woman with a straight face, I could stand behind my interview questions about race, which were not as invasive but seemed more controversial because of the subject matter.

FOOD DIARY

I have an obsessive personality. For nine straight months I ate unseasoned Westville salmon and spinach every day. Now I cannot think of anything worse (no disrespect to Westville).

My problem is that sugar is my greatest vice. I have the palate of a middle-schooler with an expense account. At seven years old, I developed an addiction to tapioca pudding. I was hyper fixated by the chewable bubbles dispersed throughout the cup, so much so that I ate a quart of tapioca pudding a day for four weeks straight. This immediately broke down my digestive system. My mother took me to my pediatrician, who diagnosed me with lactose intolerance, explaining that while most people grow intolerant with age, I was one of the rare few who made themselves intolerant through overexposure.

Each of my food obsessions demarcates a different era in my coming-of-age.

When I was coming up as a writer I was severely depressed, as opposed to now, when I am only moderately depressed. During lunch at the day job I hated, I would soothe myself by eating a donut. After work, I would eat a carton of ice cream before bed, rotating between Talenti's Raspberry Cheesecake Cookie Caramel Crunch and Ben & Jerry's Americone Dream, Netflix and Chill'd, and Brownie Batter Core. Not to stunt, but I have never in my life had a cavity. In fact, my dentist growing up used to say I had teeth like a horse, which now as an adult I realize is kind of racist, but at the time I loved my little pony. Things changed when my primary-care practitioner warned that an all-sugar diet was "very bad for me." She alleged that my Queen Frostine habit had raised my sugar levels to the point of being pre-pre-diabetic.

When [REDACTED] famously won the 2016 presidential election, I ate a combination of pad Thai, pad see ew, and drunken noodles every day for one month. To be clear, I could not afford this Seamless expenditure. Yet I had decided that ordering my body weight in Thai food would bring me a modicum of joy. It did not. However, it did almost bankrupt me.

So I turned to a new obsession.

I am constantly trying and failing to be a vegetarian because I am obsessed with saying, "Sorry, I am a vegetarian." As the child of Nigerian immigrants, I grew up with the understanding that every meal consists of carbs, vegetables, and mostly meat. Meats include but are not limited to chicken, salmon, steak, pork, goat, shrimp, and oxtail. Nigerians know their way around a butcher. But this year I made a commitment to become a vegetarian because eating less meat is better for the environment and I famously love the earth. I can usually maintain a vegetarian diet for two weeks before I falter, usually out of either iron deficiency or sheer ignorance. My biggest struggle with being a vegetarian is that I vehemently dislike the texture of beans. I hate beans. They are so mealy. Another huge impediment to becoming a vegetarian for me is that I do not know what qualifies as a vegetable. Apparently, chicken nuggets are not vegetables. Who knew? Certainly not me. I only eat two types of vegetables: spinach and asparagus. I picked up spinach because Popeye the Sailor Man lied to me as a child and said the leafy green would give me superhuman strength. And I eat asparagus because some of my most formative, deeply religious childhood memories were watching *VeggieTales*, which featured a talking asparagus named Junior.

On any given day I wonder, *What did I eat today?* That is how I structure my day. When is my next meal and what is my last meal? Is 10:00 A.M. too early for lunch? Is 4:00 P.M. too early for dinner? My life revolves around my food obsessions.

bankruptcies are caused by medical debt. This hospital was profiting off of the limits of my body. I could extend my time in the labor market, but it was going to cost, conservatively speaking, $20,000. And, this was my privilege.

When the nurse asked about my patient history, I breezed through questions about smoking, drinking, and exercise. No, no, and no. Then she asked me about any family history. I told her my mother had recently been diagnosed with cancer and then I started to sob. She apologized profusely. I couldn't make eye contact with her, instead searching the room for the rough tissues that chafed my nose. She handed me some paper towels and told me the doctor would be with me shortly.

I know why I was crying. It was the reminder that my mom was mortal, subject to the whims of her body. If that was the case for her, it was for me. She was lucky. She had adult children to help her recovery process, but what would happen to me if I chose not to have kids? Was that reason enough to bring black friends into the world? Would their bodies belong to the world? The more I ruminated on this, the more I worried that nothing I had done up until this point mattered if I didn't have a little nepo baby of my own. Ziwe Jr. deserved to capitalize on my lifetime of grunt work. If I didn't have a kid, who would inherit the fruits of my labor? Who would benefit from the lessons I learned alone in the woods or on a Jumbotron? Who would I pass on my trauma to?

Right now, my work is my child. I tuck her in every night and get her out of bed in the morning. I travel with her even though I can't stand children on planes. I worry about her when we're not together. I don't ski. I don't bike. I don't climb. I treat my body well because I'm not just living for me anymore; I'm living more for my baby—my labor.

When I was a kid, I asked my mother if I was going to get an inheritance. She handed me a Bible and said, "Thanks to me, you will inherit the Kingdom of God." To this day, I am still not entirely clear on whether I'll be getting any money. It's safe to say that answer is no. But I've gained something far more valuable: an understanding of my body's relationship to the world, passed down from my mother and her mother and her mother's mother. I don't know who will inherit my work. Or what work will be left to inherit.

Zora Neale Hurston died broke and childless, buried in an unmarked grave in a segregated cemetery. Eighty-seven years later, her novel *Their Eyes Were Watching God* started a renaissance. That's either a lonely ending or a beautiful beginning, depending on how you look at it. I'm lucky because even if I have no heir, I can appreciate that you will all take these words with you on your path. You can't have my body, but you can have my body of work.

ACKNOWLEDGMENTS

thank *you*.